Also available at all good book stores

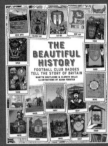

9781785317927

9781801500630

9781801500067

9781801500937

9781801500906

9781801500975

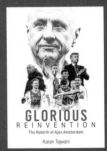

9781801500692

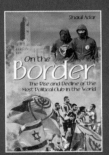

9781801500951

9781801501026

PHILOSOPHY
AND
FOOTBALL

The Story of
Philosophy Football FC

Geoff Andrews and Filippo Ricci

First published by Pitch Publishing, 2022

Pitch Publishing
9 Donnington Park,
85 Birdham Road,
Chichester,
West Sussex,
PO20 7AJ
www.pitchpublishing.co.uk
info@pitchpublishing.co.uk

ISBN 978 1 80150 099 9

Typesetting and origination by Pitch Publishing
Printed and bound in India by Replika Press Pvt. Ltd.

Contents

Prologue by Filippo Ricci

I CONSIDER Rome my city, despite being born in Reggio
Emilia, in the north of Italy, and having left the *Caput
Mundi* in 2000. In that year, I went to London to work and
I found a wonderful team to play for.

It is October 2005 and I'm in San Basilio, a working-
class district in the north-western reaches of Rome, some
distance from the Colosseum, Trevi Fountain, the Spanish

Steps and the other historic landmarks of the Eternal City. This quarter had a notorious reputation as one of the *borgate*, the urban settlements established by Mussolini in the 1930s which effectively separated these inhospitable, increasingly ghettoised suburbs from respectable Rome. In the 1970s, by which time they had seen further decay, they became a rallying point for the movement for better housing, with squatters and mass occupations drawing in a new generation of left-wing militants. At one occupation in 1974, Fabrizio Ceruso, a 19-year-old militant with the communist group Lotta Continua, was shot dead by police as they attempted to clear the buildings, spurning further demonstrations as activists converged on the district.

I had travelled from London with my team, Philosophy Football FC. On the plane there were two more Romans, a drum and bass DJ and a gastroenterologist, regulars in the PFFC squad, and the rest of the team including among them a teacher, a musician, a couple of shop managers, a film enthusiast, a Transport for London employee, an actor and a barrister. Plus there was a writer as the manager; a colourful group ranging in age from early 20s to early 40s. Before joining PFFC we didn't know each other. We had had no schools, football clubs, neighbourhoods or discos to share. Different countries, different backgrounds, different interests, different politics. We were part of the London diaspora and victims of our passion for football.

Thirty years after the strikes, occupations and police confrontations had rocked the district, things had quietened down at San Basilio, and the 60 or so people assembled at the Centro Sportivo Francesca Gianni were there to play football, not to demonstrate. It was a four-team tournament in memory of the Italian film director and writer Pier Paolo Pasolini on the 30th anniversary of his death. The location was appropriate as the Roman *borgate* had been the inspiration for several Pasolini films, including *Mamma Roma*, a masterpiece of Italian neorealist cinema which focussed on the disenfranchised and dispossessed underclass. One team, Pasoliniana, was composed, appropriately, of several of the non-professional actors from Pasolini's films; a second team was made up of prominent Italian film directors, including Matteo Garrone, who would later direct *Gomorrah* and *Dogman;* a third team, Osvaldo Soriano FC, was the Nazionale degli Scrittori, a squad of left-wing writers who took part in several writers' World Cups and were managed by Paolo Sollier, the former professional footballer who in the 1970s led Perugia's midfield in Serie A while campaigning as a militant activist of the Trotskyist group Avanguardia Operaia. Then, making up the tournament, was Philosophy Football FC. A team from London taking a break from our regular weekend matches at Regent's Park. We were immaculately turned out in blue shirts adorned with Pasolini's own words ('After literature and sex, football is one of the great pleasures'). But what was a British Sunday League team doing in Rome commemorating the life of a gay, communist Italian film director?

To answer that question this book will tell the story of a unique football team, formed in opposition to football's inequalities and from its left-wing origins had the lofty idea of returning the beautiful game to its popular, working-class roots with the mission to halt the corporate power of football. A team that in the end did not change the world or end global capitalism but welcomed more than 250 players coming from 24 different countries and six continents. A team that departed for more than 20 tours.

We met in London. A city we loved, and sometimes hated. A city that offered us opportunities, a bit of stress and a lot of bad weather. A city that provided PFFC with an incredible variety of wonderful characters, human stories and footballers. We were all looking for a team. We found friendship, fun, passion and philosophy, and were brought together by Geoff Andrews, the Gaffer. Without PFFC we wouldn't have met. With PFFC we played, travelled, ate, drank, danced and discussed – football, politics and philosophy (but always, in the end, football).

1

In Search of Philosophical Football

IT ALL started in 1994, in the midst of a significant era for British football which was still echoing to the arias of 'Nessun dorma' of Italia '90. It was in 1994 that Eric Cantona, arguably the most philosophical of footballers, who had enthralled fans in the first years of the Premier League, was voted the Professional Footballers' Association's Player of the Year, the first non-Brit to win the award since its inauguration 20 years earlier. The prospect of football reaching wider audiences had been mooted two years before with the publication of Nick Hornby's *Fever Pitch* and, for some, 1994 was the seminal moment in the modernisation of the people's game, with the introduction of all-seater stadia, and the highest attendances since 1980/81. Though it was another two years before the Arsène Wenger revolution began to transform the style and tactics of British football, the game was being enlightened by the influx of foreign players – which escalated again the following year with the introduction of the Bosman ruling – and more tactically minded coaches.

Critics would add that it was also the beginning of the 'gentrification' of football, the period in which the beautiful game became disconnected from its roots, where the corporate bosses took charge and when satellite TV started to set the agenda. Its darker side remained too, with one of Wenger's predecessors, George Graham, having to resign in the wake of a 'bung' scandal that year and one of his star players, Paul Merson, admitting his addiction to drugs and gambling. In any case, the game would never be the same again, and the story of this club is bound up with these developments.

However, the founding of Philosophy Football FC – possibly the only club to have the words 'football' appear twice in its name – has more obscure, immediate origins. These are to be found in the decline of the small British

Communist Party (CPGB) which, on the fall of the Soviet Union, called it a day in 1991 and turned itself into the short-lived Democratic Left. Three years later, Tony Blair was elected Labour leader and began his attempts to modernise his party by ditching some of its core values. Mark Perryman and Geoff Andrews had been members of the CPGB on its Eurocommunist, *Marxism Today* wing and in the aftermath of the Communist Party's demise, they met regularly as Signs of the Times, a discussion group set up and convened by Perryman which held its gatherings in a Swedish restaurant in Newington Green. Its weekly interrogation of the 'conjuncture' included such topics as postmodernism, Blairism, Europe, globalisation and the trends in popular culture. Football, they believed, was one of those cultural 'terrains' that the beleaguered left could not ignore.

In October 1994 Queens Park Rangers (Andrews' team) were a solid Premier League side and he and Perryman (a Tottenham supporter) would regularly attend matches together, albeit seated in different parts of the ground. It was after one of these, a 1-1 draw at White Hart Lane where Jürgen Klinsmann had failed to impress for the hosts and Les Ferdinand saw red for the visitors, that the post-match conversation turned to politics, football and the existentialist writer Albert Camus. Maybe the search for meaning takes on a new importance after a dull draw or perhaps Andrews and Perryman were still suffering the fall-out from the end of the CP, but in any case the two friends together with Perryman's partner, Anne Coddington (another Tottenham season-ticket holder who would later write a book on women and football, *One of the Lads*), and Tom Callaghan, a QPR-supporting friend of Andrews and a key figure in the club's early years, came up with the idea of a football shirt adorned with Camus's words, 'All that I know most surely about morality and obligation I owe to football.' By Christmas, Perryman, a brilliant organiser, catalyst and entrepreneur of left-wing causes, was selling them from his kitchen table after recruiting the talented graphic designer Hugh Tisdale to the project. The idea of Philosophy Football, 'outfitters of intellectual distinction', was born, with an impressive squad of footballers and philosophers to follow Camus.

In the meantime, Andrews began to think about the idea of a real Philosophy Football team. If starting a new squad composed entirely of philosophers was out of the question (he knew only two or three), then at least a team of 'progressive' left-wingers could be assembled. Prospects were not helped by his lack of experience. His own football career had peaked at the age of 12 as captain of his junior school team and his later experience at Oxford in the Ruskin College Second XI, and appearing for the *Marxism Today* five-a-side team in Cardiff merely marked a further descent into footballing oblivion. Nor did he have any football connections with amateur leagues, given most of his recent years had been spent in the doldrums of British left activism. Finding players for Sunday football is never easy and this was the period before emails and mobile phones.

Getting players on to the pitch was the first challenge. The second, which would take many more years to solve, was to come up with 11 players whose fitness and ability would be sufficient to avoid weekly humiliation. Following two hastily arranged and poorly attended training sessions, a team comprised of ex-communists and Democratic Left members, left-wing journalists and assorted politics, history and sociology lecturers took the pitch for the first game at Battersea Park on Sunday, 19 March 1995, the day that the other 'reds' – Liverpool and Manchester United – faced each other at Anfield. PFFC's line-up included Gareth Smyth, a journalist on *New Times*, the paper of the post-communist Democratic Left; Stefan Howald, a Swiss journalist and member of the Signs of the Times group; Dominic Ford, a Democratic Left activist; and sixth-form teachers Tom Callaghan and Imran Rahman. All of whom, along with Andrews, would play regularly in the early years. Unfortunately, Howald, at 41 and by some way PFFC's outstanding (and quickest) player, pulled a muscle in the warm-up and could only watch from the sidelines. Mark Perryman made his one and only appearance for the team, nicely turned out with new boots and exhibiting much energy, even if, like his team-mates, he rarely got near the ball. By then, Perryman and Tisdale had produced their second shirt, in honour of Bill Shankly. His socialist collectivism ('The socialism I believe in is everyone working for each other, everyone having a share of the rewards. It's the way I see football, the way I see life') appealed to the ten outfield players who wore red for the first time. Andrews wore Camus green in goal.

Unfortunately, any sartorial elegance didn't compensate for events once the match got under way. The first problem was that all the outfield players kitted out in red

Shankly wore the same number, four, a phenomenon that was unlikely to have been previously encountered by a referee had there indeed been one. The second problem was that few of the players had played 11-a-side football before. These problems were compounded when another philosopher withdrew with a thigh strain in the opening five minutes. It was only the charitable instincts of the opponents, Voluntary Services Overseas – perhaps a pointer to the club's later international adventures – that saved the team from no more than a 4-0 drubbing.

Whatever the early teething problems, there was enough goodwill and enthusiasm to continue. Hopes were raised when in the next match the team took an early 1-0 lead against Time Out, only to go down to a spirited 2-1 defeat. The recurring oddity of all the outfield players wearing the same number on their back was picked up by an *Independent* journalist, presumably covering the match in search of a new cultural trend, who commented on the confusion in the opposition ranks when team-mates were told to 'mark number four'. At least Andrews, paraphrasing Marx's 11th thesis on Feuerbach (and inscribed on his gravestone at Highgate Cemetery), was able to reassure the readership that Philosophy Football was more than a t-shirt, 'Philosophers only interpret the game; the point is to play it.'

As Andrews continued the search for philosophers who could play, the virtual squad assembled from Perryman's kitchen table in South Tottenham expanded, benefitting not only from the increasing customer base but also from the antics of the philosopher-footballer par excellence, Eric Cantona. In January 1995, Cantona had caused controversy and earned himself a ban (with community service added on) for a karate kick aimed at a Crystal Palace supporter in a Premier League match at Selhurst Park. In the ensuing media inquests, Cantona, irked by the attention his antics had brought, uttered the words, 'When the seagulls follow the trawler, it is because they think sardines will be thrown into the sea.' As the press tried to make sense of these pearls of wisdom, Perryman and Tisdale quickly got the Cantona shirt out. On the pitch, the team felt they had a common spirit.

The success of the PhilosophyFootball.com company provided a useful network for player recruitment, which would pay off in the coming years. In the short term the practicalities of getting a team out every week was still a big problem. That it was managed at all was largely due to the Andrews–Gareth Smyth partnership. Smyth, an unofficial assistant manager who had previously run another left-wing football outfit, had good links with a couple of exiled ANC-supporting South Africans who brought skill and flair to the team. He also had good connections with some of the rising New Labour entourage, including Tim Allan from the Blair press office who briefly appeared for the team; this provoked one or two philosophical discussions, though political differences seemed less significant than the skilful Allan's inability to pass to his team-mates.

Smyth had all the attributes needed of Sunday League football organisers, namely access to players and a rigid determination never to accept 'no' when seeking their availability. On the pitch he would maintain a civilised conversation with the referee, though his rallying call to his team-mates was normally confined to a quiet request to 'mark-up, gentlemen' at set pieces. He made up for lack of pace and ball skills with canny positioning and the occasional professional foul. Off the pitch, he and Andrews held protracted early morning discussions about tactics. With 4-4-2 the favoured system at the time, much attention was placed on the two central midfielders – who would have the 'holding' role? – while finding two centre-backs capable of dealing with the physical threat from Sunday League forwards was also a regular topic. Central defence would remain one of the most difficult positions to fill, made more complicated by the absence of linesmen at that level. Centre-backs had to be strong enough to deal with the physical challenges and mobile enough to cover for forward runs from offside positions. Mainly though, these tactical discussions remained at an abstract level: getting 11 players on the pitch was always the priority at this time.

Nevertheless, with the arrival of some better players and despite some more friendly thrashings – 6-3 to St Bartholomew's Hospital, and 8-2 to Hoxton Pirates – over the summer, the team entered the Musical Association League Division Two for the 1995/96 season. The choice of the Musical Association League (set up by Radio 1 celebrities in 1984 and still in existence today) was mainly on the grounds that it seemed the 'friendliest' league available. It was only later that the team recruited some musicians and distributed an annual CD among the squad. Home matches were to be played at Regent's Park. Though PFFC's home pitch would change over the years, Regent's Park remained the spiritual base for many of the team and the venue for some of its finest – and most forgettable – moments. It was also a very convenient location. Unlike conventional Sunday League teams which were normally formed by players from the same locality, or the midweek work- and office-based teams, PFFC always drew on players from across London, the majority of whom had moved to the capital for work. As the team developed over the years, its main identity would be as a team of adopted Londoners, symptomatic of the modern London diaspora.

The transition to regular league football was not a success. Despite an unexpected early home point in a 2-2 draw, PFFC were on the receiving end of a series of heavy losses: 11-0 and 7-1 to St Pauli, the eventual champions, and 6-1 to Cobra Sports, among them. PFFC had only one point by Christmas. The team had to wait until the beginning of February for its first victories in an unexpected purple patch, when it followed a 5-2 league win with an unlikely act of cup giant-killing in defeating Apollo XI, from the exalted heights of the Musical Association League Division One. The 4-3 result, in a bad-tempered if exciting affair, ended with PFFC holding on despite two late goals. This abrupt change of fortune was largely due to the acquisition of a new young Cypriot forward, Billi – but nicknamed Romario – whose goalscoring exploits brought a new dimension to the team. His appearance also necessitated a change in formation that temporarily proved successful; a 4-5-1, capable of quickly switching to 5-4-1 as required. These victories were fleeting moments, a temporary respite against a wider trend of mediocrity. Keith Williams, a Liverpudlian primary school teacher who played on the left wing in front of Andrews at full-back, once scored a spectacular goal from inside his own half at Maida Vale only to see his team lose 10-1.

Odd victories apart, PFFC's first full season was proving to be more than a challenge. Regular Sunday morning matches (and occasional afternoon fixtures) represented a commitment many were unprepared for, while the routines and practices of Sunday League football came as a culture shock. The physical side took its toll on ageing players, who faced the added difficulty of having to adapt to both grass and astroturf. The dressing rooms at Regent's Park often resembled a mud bath in the race to get into the showers under the strict orders of the matriarch in charge who always turned the hot water off promptly at 4pm; on one occasion, later described in Pete May's book *Sunday Muddy Sunday*, PFFC players were left literally in a cold sweat with mud trickling down their knees as the clock ticked past four.

In addition to Regent's Park, PFFC also played home matches at Caledonian Road in Islington and Paddington Rec, Maida Vale, both astroturf surfaces, which left their marks. Stefan Howald, a remarkably fit and agile forward who would continue playing for PFFC into his mid-50s, was one of several who would regularly leave the pitch with cuts to the knees and arms. In his case, the application of *grappa*, from the Ticino (Italian-speaking) region of Switzerland, by his partner Renee, was found to be the best solution.

Some of the exchanges on the pitch were another eye-opener for the team. Even in a friendly league the banter in Sunday football is not for the faint-hearted and for a while PFFC was outshouted and undone by more skilful, physical and streetwise opponents. Referees, who always seemed to have a thankless and poorly rewarded task – one of the main managerial roles at this level was to sort out a ref for home matches – could often be swayed by vocal opponents, which was not PFFC's style. Where other teams might hurl abuse at the referee for not awarding a penalty, Tom Callaghan would pick the ball up and with quiet irony place it on the penalty spot before calmly retreating to his position as right-back. His quiet, quizzical response to the possibility of any fracas – 'are you calling me a Kant?' – was lost on opponents. The team struggled throughout the season, but did at least receive a trophy, awarded perhaps as much to gratitude from the opponents for the easy wins, as well as a little genuine affection. It was inscribed, 'Gone to the dogs. Bottom of the League. Philosophy Football'.

By the end of the first season, PhilosophyFootball.com had expanded its range of shirts – adding the likes of Brian Clough, postmodernist Jean Baudrillard and the Italian Marxist Antonio Gramsci – and Perryman, Tisdale and their team of volunteers had organised a major event on London's South Bank, titled Europe United, to coincide with Euro '96. The event included a 'Football Fashion Show' in the Purcell Room Foyer, a 'European Fans Forum', a two-man revue on 'The Complete History of the World Cup', one-man show on Albert Camus and a men's and women's four-a-side football tournament organised by PFFC which was held on the ground floor of the Royal Festival Hall, with two pillars in the centre of the pitch. Their opponents included the Zapatistas, the Half-Time Oranges and Fantasy Football. In a crunch match against the latter, Graham

Kelly, the FA's chief executive, guesting for PFFC on the day and kitted out in an Antonio Gramsci shirt, scored one of the goals in a 2-1 victory. Among the on-looking supporters, David Dein, then Arsenal vice-chairman, was heard to chant 'there's only one Graham Kelly'.

That event proved to be a welcome respite from the weekly exertion which now resembled some of the typical characteristics of a Sunday League team. However interesting and different the team was in personnel and in its noble attempt to be something different from the everyday rituals of Sunday League football, it is not much fun if you lose every week. This was despite the fact that over the course of the season the Philosophy Football network had continued to bring in some interesting players. Nicholas Royle, an aspiring novelist, had offered his services as a goalkeeper who had actually read Camus. Given PFFC already had a keeper, and with his short stature in mind, Royle was quickly converted into a tenacious, tough-tackling right-back. For each home match, Royle would be seen arriving at Regent's Park with his head in a book; he seemed the ideal recruit. In later years, as novelist, short story writer and lecturer, he would reach the heights of the England Writers' team. However, his PFFC career was cut short. By the end of the first season, Royle, who had originally been 'poached' from Time Out (one of PFFC's early friendly opponents), had become disillusioned by the despondency which marked every defeat, and was 'relieved' when the early morning calls stopped coming. 'They were the least philosophical team I've ever played in,' he wrote in a later *New Statesman* diary item. 'In defeat, that is. Took it very badly. Even talked about training sessions. No thank you. Not my idea of Sunday football.'

The loss of Gareth Smyth, who left for the Middle East for a prolific career as journalist and editor, initially in Beirut and then Tehran (where he was the *Financial Times* correspondent) at the end of that year, was a severe blow and it appeared to Andrews that the team was a long way from reconciling the thoughts of Albert Camus with the difficulties of dealing with pacy forwards on a wet Sunday morning. The routines and the defeats were taking their toll on the manager. Andrews was disillusioned and stood down at the end of the season, leaving Dom Ford, the first in a long line of Liverpudlian centre-backs, in charge, ably assisted by Tom Callaghan, Imran Rahman and Stefan Howald. Over the next three seasons, Philosophy Football continued as a Sunday League team, winning more matches but developing little of a philosophical identity. It shared the problems that all Sunday League teams face at one time or the other: a continual and sometimes losing struggle to get a full team out. The following year started in the same way as the inaugural season with heavy defeats to the likes of West XI, Cobra and Red Star Camden (10-1 on ice, in the cup). In many of the games PFFC started with nine or fewer players, with its obvious effects on team spirit. Nevertheless, a couple of late wins and a walkover (awarded when the opponents don't show) ensured an improvement to second from bottom.

The 1997/98 season saw Imran Rahman in charge following Dom Ford's departure. Rahman was a skilful player who served the team in a variety of positions. He was probably best in the centre of midfield, where as one of the few naturally gifted players at that time he bore resemblance to the later Luka Modrić, spreading passes and cajoling his team-mates to ever greater endeavours. He demanded the same levels of passionate commitment from others as he expended himself. This was a battle he ultimately couldn't win, however. Getting 11 players on the pitch remained a major hurdle and indeed also affected some of PFFC's opponents. The season featured the usual mix of heavy defeats, narrow victories and the occasional walkover. At one of their last fixtures that season, the players arrived at Regent's Park on a warm spring afternoon to find their opponents already engaged in another match. They had fallen behind with their games and had to make up by playing back-to-back. Well-beaten and exhausted after the first match they nevertheless managed to beat PFFC in their second. The team was as far away as it had been from marrying football with philosophy. At the end of the year, the United Nations of Football, another big alternative football event organised by Perryman and Tisdale on the South Bank, offered a further reminder of the growing divergence between the pleasures of Philosophy Football off the pitch and the pains of Philosophy Football FC on it.

The following season started as before with bad-tempered affairs, cup exits and the last-minute recruitment of players from the park to make up the numbers. In its first match PFFC again had to recruit three players from the touchline and trailed to Black Vinyl Hearts by the break. It was too much for Stefan Howald, who quit in disgust at half-time. It was a clear signal of decline and by the end of that season PFFC found itself with neither a team nor a philosophy.

The following season, 1999/2000, partly encouraged by the success of PhilosophyFootball.com, whose range of shirts and events had expanded, Andrews started again: determined this time to unite philosophy and football. He had some mild optimism that the organisational burden could be reduced. Mobile phones had arrived and some players even had email addresses. The days of leaving late-night phone messages with flat-mates or on the answerphones of players' girlfriends was hopefully over. With Howald and Callaghan the only continuing players, new recruits were found via the Philosophy Football newsletter, the *New Statesman* and *When Saturday Comes*. Tony Batt, a Tottenham-supporting web designer who had carried out work for the Philosophy Football company, joined on the precondition there would be no training. He was promptly made captain of the new-look team. Batt, an admirer of Robin Friday, the wayward, undisciplined, skilful forward for Reading and Cardiff – one of England's greatest football misfits – played in a variety of roles in the team until fitness got the better of him. Simon Carmel, an academic and another utility man who could play anywhere across the defence, became a reliable player and an even more expert scout for the team. He was responsible for bringing in two of PFFC's most important players: Paul Kayley, who would captain the team in its most successful period, and Alan Johns, a Cornish barrister who, as a tricky winger in the old-fashioned mode, once had a trial for Lou Macari's Swindon, and belonged to the same church as

Carmel. A third Carmel recruit, Mark 'Goober' Fox, would play a key role off the pitch in sustaining the club's website over the best part of two decades.

Kayley, a computer programmer, had recently moved to London from the north-west. Though he was a regular five-a-side player he had played little 11-a-side and had been put off by the culture of pub football. Turning up for a friendly he was both impressed by the civility and mix of his new team-mates as well as surprised to find that, in his early 30s, he was one of the youngest players in the team. Andrews was in his late 30s, Callaghan was in his early 40s (as was Danny Burke, a friend he had brought to the team), and Howald by this time was in his late 40s.

Despite these new recruits, things would get worse before they improved. This makeshift outfit, in the process of being rebuilt, still relied on getting additional players – a girlfriend's brother, a work-mate, friend of a friend, sometimes recruiting players hanging about on the sidelines – in order to get a team out. The problems with this strategy for a team with philosophical as well as football ambitions, erupted one afternoon in east London – in what was later to be known in club folklore as 'The Battle of Mile End', where insults and punches were thrown on both sides, red cards were issued and the game was abandoned. Andrews was mortified and only persuaded to carry on after several pints of Guinness in the post-mortem held in the pub afterwards. Things would have to change.

He decided that from now on there could be no compromises on philosophy. The Philosophy Football network was still expanding and there was the chance to recruit more like-minded players. Never a party political concern, PFFC was stumbling towards a shared ethos broad enough to accommodate Johns (promptly nicknamed 'Cornish Al'), who had recently become a committed Christian and was conservatively minded in politics, and Raj Chada, a defence lawyer and future Labour leader of Camden Council, who turned up one Sunday in his Shankly shirt. A tough-tackling midfielder, he and Johns, both in their mid-20s and then the youngest players in the team, would form one of the key partnerships as PFFC sought to rebuild.

The team needed a new goalkeeper. Previously filled by 'Greek Andy', one of Gareth Smyth's recruits, and occasionally by Andrews himself, it was a key position. Renowned for their individuality and eccentricity, and often a law unto themselves, getting the right person was crucial. Vassilis Fouskas, a university colleague of Andrews, had been a former goalkeeper from the lower levels of the Greek professional league. He seemed a perfect addition. At well over six feet tall, Fouskas initially intimidated his team-mates with his vigorous warm-up routines but then had them in awe by somehow reaching a shot destined for the top corner. For some time after, 'that save' would be recounted by those who saw it. However, Fouskas was the antithesis of the many academics who had recently become enraptured by football. Having seen the corrupt side of the game in Greece, he now had little interest in football and was totally committed to his academic career (later becoming a politics professor).

Rob Adams had been one half of the two-man revue on the history of the World Cup at the Europe United event three years earlier, though was then unknown to Andrews. He had turned out a bit in goal for Sporting Hackney Second XI but was struck by PFFC's eclectic ad in *When Saturday Comes*. Adams, an actor and drama teacher, would play for the club for the next 20 years, when he was well into his 50s. His PFFC career nearly ended on its first day, however. On arrival at Regent's Park for his first game against London Weekend Television, he only paid the parking meter until half-time, a situation which unnerved his manager.

Adams, along with Johns, Chada, Kayley, Fox and other new recruits had been vital in building a camaraderie among the players, which for some time after continued to compensate for poor results on the pitch. Heavy defeats meant another bottom-of-the table finish was guaranteed from early on, with their one league victory, achieved in a late-season clash against a team also at the wrong end of the table, a moment for celebration. The team, with several players over 40, was beginning to enjoy itself at least, and held its first election of player of the year (won by Adams, by now 'Rob the Cat' after brilliant individual performances) over borsch, duck and vodka at Patio, a Polish restaurant in Shepherd's Bush.

This new spirit of unity was strengthened when Stefan Howald, through his contacts in Zurich, organised PFFC's first European football tour in June 2000. Before moving to London as a correspondent for his Swiss newspaper, Howald had played for FC Levante Wibi, which had been founded in the 1970s by an anarchist collective. Now he took equal pride in introducing his team-mates to his city and his old team to his London squad of philosophers. After the team had assembled at Luton Airport for the first of what would be many early morning flights on the low-cost airlines, they were met in Zurich by their host and veteran striker, who took them on a tour of the old town, posing for photos outside Lenin's old house and stopping at sights and bars along the way. The accommodation provided by their opponents included a commune, which caused confusion for some of the players on the way home that evening who found themselves lost in a neighbouring apartment.

The next day, a tactical team talk over brunch was followed by an early arrival at the sports ground for the match. The pitch was a step up from what the team had previously encountered. Beautiful surroundings, a decent-sized crowd and convivial, like-minded opponents. Training was still anathema to most of the squad but some limbering-up exercises were carried out on the outskirts of the pitch. The team's traditional red colours had been supplemented by the company's navy training tops, adorned with each individual player's initials. The match itself, played in a great spirit, yielded yet another defeat (4-0), despite some promising moves. Congratulations were offered by both captains and Andrews made an impromptu speech extolling the virtues of European unity. The post-match fraternising carried on long into the night. As the first PFFC tour, the experience made a lasting impression on Andrews, and suggested that Europe could be the answer to the club's search for an identity. He could not have foreseen the ways in which this would become a reality, from the changing composition of the squad to the style of football and even the post-match food.

However, there remained one outstanding matter that needed urgent attention. He knew from experience that however harmonious the team appeared to be, you could only keep losing for a limited time before players became disillusioned. Plus, there seemed to be a perennial question at the back of his mind, which had troubled many philosophers though presumably few who had managed football teams. In building a different kind of team, where do you draw the line between philosophy and praxis? Or, put another way, to what extent do you compromise your principles for the sake of getting three points on the board? He felt he had only half a team – Adams, Johns, Chada, Kayley and Howald – with the necessary quality and fitness to be competitive on a weekly basis. The search was on for the others.

2

An Italian Earthquake

ZURICH HAD suggested that a new beginning for the club was possible. Most Sunday League teams end their 90 minutes of battle in the mud with a quick pint afterwards for the hardened regulars. Others slip off with barely time for a change of clothes. Few get the chance of a European tour. The players took to it, relished the experience, and wanted more. The tour had strengthened the bonds between like-minded individuals and had broadened the vision of what the team could aspire to be, while maintaining a commitment to an alternative idea of football: one that promoted conviviality, fair play and (now) internationalism. For Andrews, however, any new identity, even a new *philosophy*, would only survive if the occasional victory was on the horizon. If the next league season was to avoid the calamity of the previous year, then younger and better players were needed. More than that, the club now needed to be on a stronger footing and, if regular training was destined to be a never-to-be-attained utopia, then some tighter organisation was going to be crucial.

PFFC prepared for the 2000/01 season with a big recruitment campaign via the PhilosophyFootball.com newsletter and *When Saturday Comes*. Andrews introduced some new rules. Every player now had to have an email address. If PFFC was to be sustainable beyond another season, then players would need to embrace its values and turn up each week. From then on, the team was primarily organised through an email list, with Monday notices asking for availability and Wednesday for confirmation of the squad and the venue details for the Sunday morning fixture. Players were instructed to be at the ground 45 minutes before kick-off. The previous group of disparate individuals was to be replaced by a stronger collective entity. One player was designated to do the match report (which became a regular PFFC feature, along with an end-of-season review) and each player was required to look after and wash their own shirts. Only red PF shirts were permissible (for home kits); no commercial Coca-Cola or other makeshift attire was to be tolerated. The line-up was to be selected on merit, not according to how long a player had been playing for the team or some other favourable circumstance. Once the minimum commitment was established, the manager must have the discretion to select the best team. Central to this strategy, of course, was having more than 11 players to choose from.

The email list proved to be an important management tool and increased Andrews' authority by reducing his organisational burden. There were a few teething problems, however. Owen Mather, who would go on to be the club's most capped player, was one of the young recruits during the summer of 2000. He had moved to London from Preston, Lancashire, 18 months before and had known about Philosophy Football from the shirt advertisements and had even worn a Shankly top in a students versus tutors football match at the University of Central Lancashire (the lecturers wore Baudrillard and Nietszche). Working in a call centre prior to starting a PGCE at Greenwich, Mather knew few people in London apart from his house-mates and was only made aware of the team when his mother forwarded on the PF newsletter. His attempts to join were nearly thwarted by Andrews' new measures as he was not on email, and despite sending a complete footballing CV from school age onwards his aspiration to join the team was initially rebuffed by the manager's new regime. Eventually, a compromise was agreed whereby for the next season Mather's boss would receive the emailed match information, print it out each week and leave it on his desk in time for him to reply by the required date. This did not always go to plan. 'OK, that's it. I've had it!!! Please please please stop clogging up my inbox with this stuff. No more political theorising or philosophical debate. Interesting though it may be,' an irate boss responded after one frenetic build-up of PFFC email traffic.

Mather was one of the 'class of 2000' who would be crucial to the development of the club. Another who joined at this time was Jeremy (Jez) Bray who, like Mather, was recruited thanks to the initiative of his mum. She was on the PF mailing list after buying him the Camus shirt, and promptly alerted him. Bray, a scientist, had recently arrived in London from Bath to take up a job investigating mad cow disease (BSE) at the Ministry of Agriculture. Like Mather, Bray came from a Liverpool-supporting family. His father, Ken Bray, a theoretical physicist, would go on to write two books that might have been of some use to his son's new team, which promised to 'reveal the science behind the beautiful game': *How to Score a Goal* and *How to Take a Penalty*. Bray was the same age as Mather and, at 24, they significantly reduced the average age of the team.

Joe Boyle, an online editor on the *Daily Express*, had turned out for the team a couple of times the previous season and now became a regular. He had recently moved to London from spells in rural parts of East Anglia and smaller English university towns. Like others, playing for PFFC aided his integration into the capital. He was intrigued by the advert in the *New Statesman*, which hinted at a team that was 'left-field, probably not too good for this not too good player'.

The influx of players included Richard Shepherd, a part-time actor, well over six feet tall, and with an athletic frame that would provide much-needed pace and power. He also had an enormously long throw, a useful weapon for any Sunday League team and a match for Rory Delap, then Derby County's Irish midfielder. Film-maker Keir Husband, a short and stocky Scottish midfielder, had the political heritage and the footballing nous (and build) of Charlie Adam to help the team become more consistent and competitive.

To consolidate this new beginning, Andrews had entered PFFC for a new league for the 2000/01 season. The Grafton Millennium League was a newly established friendly competition set up by Barry McNamara, an unlikely gentleman footballer and stalwart of the Sunday game. This meant a host of new away venues, mainly along the outer fringes of the Northern Line and beyond, with away fixtures at East Ewell, Worcester Park and Hampton Court, as well as nearer options in Dulwich and Colliers Wood. The prospect of travelling beyond the parameters of the London A-Z while aiming to be more competitive certainly meant that some transformation was needed.

This was indeed what happened, though the change came from an unlikely source and in ways that were unimaginable at the time. In February of that year the Italian football journalist Filippo Ricci was in Accra, Ghana, to cover his fourth African Cup of Nations. As one of a small European press contingent, he quickly got to know a couple of English journalists, Conrad Leach and Ian Coyne. Coyne, after recently completing a master's degree in African studies at Edinburgh University (with a dissertation on sport under apartheid), had opted for a career as a football reporter and was pleased to meet Ricci. The three of them started hanging out together, attending games and press conferences, meeting for dinner and playing the odd game of pool in a Ghanaian bar.

Ricci and Benedetta Mascalchi, his wife, were already thinking about a move from Rome to London, where there were better career prospects for football correspondents, while she was interested in pursuing a career as a football photographer. Ricci had always loved English football. In Rome he was still turning out for Tottenham 90, a team made up of a group of close friends which was slowly making its way from the eighth to the sixth division of the local league. At school at the age of ten he was nicknamed Phil Neal, after the Liverpool defender who had scored the third goal in their victory over Borussia Mönchengladbach in the final of the European Cup, played at Rome's Stadio Olimpico in 1977.

On moving to London, therefore, he was adamant he would find a football team. He renewed his contact with Ian Coyne, who told him he had just joined an interesting outfit after spotting an advert for the team in a magazine. He told Ricci that they seemed a nice bunch and wore interesting shirts with quotes from philosophers. Ricci had heard about the Philosophy Football shirts and in fact already owned three (Camus, Cantona and Bob Marley), given to him the previous year in lieu of payment for his articles in *When Saturday Comes*. Ricci's mother had been a philosophy teacher, and for that reason it was a subject he normally avoided. However, this wouldn't be too much of a problem, he thought. He was intrigued by the team and excited by the prospect of playing in the shirts.

After he and Benedetta arrived in London on 19 September, the day after Chelsea appointed Claudio Ranieri as their new manager following the dismissal of another Italian, Gianluca Vialli, he called Coyne and asked if there was any chance of getting a run-out with the team. 'We have a game in Regent's Park this Sunday,' Coyne told him. On Sunday, 24 September his long association with the club began with a friendly at what would become one of his favourite places in London. Regent's Park was one of a cluster of royal parks originally appropriated by King Henry VIII for hunting purposes. It was designed in its modern form by John Nash, architect to the crown in the 18th century, who, under the influence of his friend the Prince Regent, arranged it around a lake and a canal. The public were only admitted to the park in the 19th century, when it was still the preserve of the wealthy residents from nearby villas, but by the early 21st century its elegant landscape, which covers 197 hectares, provided a range of public amenities including a zoo and the largest grass sports area in central London.

And at the heart of this huge arena were ten football pitches. In Rome, where most amateur matches were played on clay, this was a revelation to Ricci. It was a perfect introduction and as he watched the first half from the touchline in typical London drizzle, he was reminded of the romantic attractions of English football. Over the following six years some of these illusions would be slowly dismantled and on that first Sunday he got an early glimpse of what was to come. Unusually, his arrival coincided with a full squad on the back of PFFC's heavy recruitment campaign and he spent his first match in the London rain (which later turned into a hailstorm) watching his team-mates play out an honourable 2-2 draw in their first fixture of the new league against Grafton FC. At least it gave him an idea of what was to come: long balls, misplaced short passes, strong tackles (most of them of the sliding variety) and a type of header unheard of in Italy.

After an avalanche of requests to join PFFC, almost too many for him to handle or sort by email, Andrews was not looking to take any more players at that time. But Filippo made an immediate impression on him. His Italian background resonated with Andrews, who enjoyed Italian football, had studied Italian politics at university and was a follower of the Italian Marxist intellectual Antonio Gramsci. It was another important European connection. Ricci was invited to play in the next match the following week when PFFC were back at Regent's Park for a friendly. Ricci and Coyne could only play the first half as they had to get to Stamford Bridge to report on Claudio Ranieri's first home game in charge against Liverpool (Chelsea won 3-0 with the help of young Italian debutant Sam Dalla Bona). When Ricci and Coyne left, PFFC were trailing 2-1 in what looked to be another encouraging performance. However, in a second half reminiscent of earlier calamities, they succumbed to a 12-1 defeat. Andrews' brief report on the game the next day made no mention of the score, perhaps mindful of upsetting a promising start to the league campaign. It was only a friendly after all. However, Ricci, who had to ask persistently for confirmation of the final score, was shocked, not only at the result but at the apparent downplaying of its importance. This was something he had not experienced in Italy where the result was all-important, and while he was prepared to adjust to the peculiarities of his new country, it was a little disturbing. Something would have to be done.

Despite the 12-1 drubbing, PFFC continued to be competitive in their next league game – Filippo's full debut – against Strollers, the reigning Grafton League champions. This was a tough test and having lived up to their name by arriving late from Wimbledon, Strollers – 'pleasant enough off the pitch, not too jolly on it' as Boyle's match report put it – fell behind after a slick move between Johns and Chada resulted in the latter's first PFFC goal. Tackles were flying and tempers flared but PFFC held out until the second half when two quick goals put Strollers in front. Was this the sign of another collapse? Ricci and his team-mates rallied, and a late equaliser seemed a just reward for a spirited performance. An unbeaten start to the league against strong opponents suggested a corner had been turned and maybe Ricci's early concerns that he had joined a squad devoid of the necessary commitment had been answered.

The team had to wait for another month for their next fixture against the high-flying (and eventual champions) South Indies. Their first away match was to be played at Market Road in Islington, on one of the first astroturf pitches to be built in London. PFFC had played on this surface in previous years and some players had dark memories of heavy defeats. For Ricci, who was enjoying the grass of Regent's Park, the surface was the first problem in what became a difficult match for him and the team. He thought the term 'astroturf' was misleading. The pitch was very worn and faded; its original green colour had turned into a greyish mess which matched London's late autumn skies. It was also very hard: more like cement covered with a light carpet. This made for irregular passages of play and, from his position as a right-footed left-back, he had to deal with long balls from the opposition which could reach the penalty area in two bounces. A new language, a new country and now a type of football which seriously questioned all that he had learned about the beautiful game. Yet it was the words of a British football manager, Brian Clough, emblazoned on a Philosophy Football shirt worn that day by PFFC's skipper (an Evertonian who refused to wear Shankly) that summed up Ricci's predicament, 'If God had wanted football to be played in the air he would have put grass [or in this case astroturf] in the sky.'

His biggest problem was to come. Playing in front of him in midfield was another of PFFC's summer recruits, who had made his mark by scoring the late equaliser in the previous game against Strollers. On the pitch he played wide on the left. Off the pitch, he was even further to the left. In the weeks since joining he had raised some eyebrows by demanding, with Leninist precision, regular training sessions and maximum attendance. Andrews, an ex-communist, was already wondering if this Troublesome Trot was entirely suited to PFFC's philosophy. Now things came to a head. After the umpteenth long ball came his way, Ricci attempted to bring it under control but only managed to divert it into touch, incurring a hostile riposte from his left-wing team-mate. A mini fracas followed, when with what British football commentators refer to as 'handbags' were exchanged. A bit of pushing and shoving, and a stand-off between the two. Ricci had always accepted that he was not the most technically gifted of Italian players and that his strengths lay in carrying out some of the hard graft to enable more skilful players to perform. But here he was in a new situation when even doing the basics on such a surface was a challenge. On the other hand, the Troublesome Trot was a skilful winger who was not always attentive to his defensive responsibilities. Each blamed the other. Other PFFC players stood around not knowing how to react. As manager, Andrews had to make a choice between the two. It was not such a hard decision for he had warmed to Ricci in recent weeks and could already see the many positive benefits he had brought to the team. He could see that Ricci's charisma was helping to change the culture and mentality of the football club in a way that strengthened its identity. He could see his influence on the other players: they were willing to take on board his ideas and were motivated by the new energy he had brought to the team.

It was a pivotal moment, nonetheless, and Andrews substituted the TT and subsequently removed him from the team. For his part, Ricci felt that he had won the trust of the manager and his team-mates and although the match was lost 3-1, he felt an important milestone had been reached in his attempts to adapt to British Sunday League football.

He still had some way to go, however, in fully adjusting to the norms of the game. The following week PFFC made the long journey along the south London perimeter of the A-Z for the first encounter of what would be a regular rivalry with Inter Aztec, a no-nonsense, physical and competitive squad who already had their eye on the Grafton League trophy. They were organised and prepared and even provided a match programme for their opponents. A nice touch. The long journey was a challenge for some of the PFFC squad and Andrews had to make a rare start at left-back, with Coyne still struggling to make kick-off. Nevertheless, they had the best of a goalless first half. In a tense affair PFFC then took the lead with a scrambled goal from full-back Boyle, only for Aztec to equalise with a piece of individual brilliance from their substitute. The momentum seemed to be with the home side and Adams had to make a couple of sharp saves.

Two things then occurred. Andrews, who by now had substituted himself, switched to a 3-5-2, moving the late-arriving Coyne to a central midfield role. The second thing that happened was that Ricci, playing in a more advanced position in the new formation, was getting frustrated and, after a rare sojourn into the unfamiliar territory of the opponents' penalty box, 'went down a little too easily' (as British football pundits put it) accompanied by anguished cries. The referee was not impressed, but his reaction paled in comparison to three of the Aztec players who, uttering expletives and with raised fists, chased Ricci to the touchline in a scene reminiscent of the Keystone Cops. Ricci's team-mates were also shocked by the episode and were as nonplussed as the referee.

It was some years before 'simulation' was deemed a mandatory yellow card and, in under-stated British fashion, the game carried on with no reprimands for the culprit or his persecutors. Yet, something had changed. It was the turning point of the match, as Aztec were ruffled and unsettled by the incident. Two goals from Richard Shepherd and Chris Smithers sealed a PFFC victory. After the match Ricci attempted to explain his actions to his team-mates and insisted on writing the match report. He needed to make a point. PFFC were on top but they needed to show steel, that determination to win, including, if necessary, by adopting some questionable tactics. Here was a clash of cultures in the land of 'fair play'. 'It's not easy to erase 20 years of Italian football within just three games on the island,' he pleaded with his team-mates. He pointed out that, back home, to be *furbo,* that is crafty or devious, is seen as a virtue. This is because – he ended his match report – in Italian, 'Nel calcio contano solo i risultati.' In football, it is only the result that counts.

In *The Dark Heart of Italy*, Tobias Jones, a British writer living in Parma (who turned out for a local Italian team), suggested:

'Comparing Italian and British football (not necessarily at the top level, but down the divisions) is like comparing snooker with darts. One is cerebral, stylish, slipping the ball across the smooth green felt; the other a bit overweight, slightly raucous, throwing the occasional arrow in the right direction.

'Talk to any Italian about the strengths of the Italian game, and they will always mention the two vital ingredients lacking in Britain: *fantasia* and *furbizia* – fantasy and cunning. Fantasy is the ability to do something entirely unpredictable with the ball. The British, I'm endlessly told, will always try to pass through a defence, or run past it, but they never actually outwit it. That's what Italian fantasists do: they produce a nanosecond of surprise that springs open a defence.'

Ricci would never dive again in PFFC colours. Despite the cultural differences, his team-mates had warmed to his personality and he was a valued member of the squad both on and off the pitch. For Ricci, finding a football team had been crucial in his wider integration into London life. He also wanted to reciprocate and enable PFFC to experience real Italian football. A little over two months after joining the team, he discussed with Andrews the possibility of playing a fixture in Rome.

3

All Roads Lead to Rome

THE ROME trip – PFFC's first of several tours to the Italian capital – would be a good test and another opportunity for the players to cement their European identity. Plus, Filippo would have a little pride in bringing his British football team home and showing them his city. The match had to be right and things needed to be done properly. As a football-mad country, Italy hosted an array of teams across the different professions and its national team of journalists held regular fixtures. As a former squad member and son of a previous manager of the Nazionale Giornalisti, Ricci was still in touch with them. Their numbers included his old schoolfriend Luigi Coldagelli, press officer to Walter Veltroni, an MP who would become the mayor of Rome the following year. In six weeks, Ricci organised the match, venue and accommodation and Andrews assembled the squad for the weekend trip in mid-December.

At the hotel near Heathrow, where some of the squad spent the night before their early flight, he had much to contemplate. He had had a good response to his call for the tour, with most of the players on their first PFFC trip and eager to follow Filippo's trail. They left in good form. The previous week PFFC had thrashed Burge and Gunson, the bathroom fitters from Colliers Wood, with hat-tricks from Chris Smithers and Stefan Howald in the 7-1 win. In addition to Rob Adams, Alan Johns and Raj Chada who had been in Zurich, Joe Boyle, Owen Mather, Jez Bray, Ian Coyne, Richard Shepherd and Smithers, a quiet Canadian centre-forward, made up a strong squad ranging in age from 23 to 39 and composed of four journalists, a trainee teacher, two part-time actors, two lawyers, a young scientist and an academic. Andrews had also been promised the temporary services of Matteo Patrono who worked for Italy's left-wing newspaper *Il Manifesto* and apparently was a useful centre-back. With Ricci himself, that made up the 11 with the by now semi-retired Andrews the only substitute. Still, he was apprehensive. It was a big ask to expect this squad, a new mix of players mostly unknown to each other three months before and which had only recently begun to avoid calamitous defeats, to hold their own against experienced opponents. A sleepless night ensued for him, which was particularly unwelcome given the match was to kick off within three hours of their arrival at Rome's Fiumicino airport.

The venue could not have been better, if only adding to the daunting prospect of the match ahead. La Borghesiana was a beautiful complex of sports and social facilities used by Italy's national football team; the equivalent of Bisham Abbey, the manor house and sports ground used by the England team. It was some contrast with the sloping recreation ground in south London where they had played their last fixture. There were plush dressing rooms, a practice arena, two linesmen, corner flags and – as Joe Boyle later recounted – 'a pitch so smooth they could cut it into strips, roll it up and sell it as lavatory paper'. Pleasingly for Andrews, there was a proper dugout complete with roof.

In the build-up to the match Andrews and Ricci held long conversations about formation and tactics. They had decided, partly with damage-limitation in mind, to opt for a more defensive 4-4-1-1, with Alan Johns in the number ten role behind Chris Smithers (in the absence of Stefan Howald) and with the two banks of four situated in a trench-like 'war of position', under strict orders to get behind the ball at the earliest opportunity. Pace was something PFFC did have, for once, as the younger if technically more limited of the two teams, and they made a bright start with good interplay from Johns and Smithers, only to be undone by a ferocious 30-yard piledriver into the top corner. Undeterred however, and perhaps still wondering how on earth they could be enjoying such splendid surroundings on a sunny Friday afternoon in December, Jez Bray soon equalised, slamming in a rebound after a shot by Shepherd was parried by their goalkeeper. This was an inspiring performance and Andrews (who made a brief ten-minute cameo appearance while Ricci took a break) was moved by the response of his team. They had quickly settled into a new formation and their swift breaks were causing problems. In one of these, just on half-time, Smithers pounced for his seventh goal in eight games. Ironically, for all their opponents' tactical superiority, it was an unorthodox British version of catenaccio, a classic Italian tactic of deep defending and quick counter-attacking, that was winning.

Half-time brought a tactical change for the Italians, who switched to a 3-5-2 formation to allow their playmaker more space to assert his influence. More resolute defending suggested an unlikely PFFC victory was possible, but with five minutes to go Luigi, Filippo's old school-mate, went down in the penalty area after Raj Chada made a last-ditch lunge of the type that regularly escapes punishment in the mud of Regent's Park. The resulting penalty struck the upright and the backside of Rob Adams before dribbling over the line. It was a late blow, but overall the match was a big moral victory for PFFC, who were unperturbed by the loss of a hastily arranged penalty shoot-out.

The match itself was only one part of a memorable, eventful and transformative weekend. On the way to the post-match meal that evening, two of the squad (Boyle and Johns), having become estranged from the rest in search of a *vineria* in Campo dei Fiori, found themselves held up by sirens, outriders and what looked to Johns to be a 'cavalcade'. 'It's not a cavalcade,' Boyle replied. 'It's the Pope-mobile.' Pope John Paul II, not in the best of health in his last years and engulfed by cassock and cardinals, had embarked on an unexpected early evening parade for his devotees.

In Campo dei Fiori, there were more surprises for the squad – with the exception of Smithers, whose mother had claimed him for her tour of Europe – with glasses of local red wine replacing the pub fayre of Camden Town. Later, over a large table in a nearby trattoria, Ricci was host and conductor of ceremonies, guiding the players through the different courses as the various episodes of the match and first live impressions of Italian football (and its officiating) were revisited over *supplì*, pasta and artichokes. The team bonded in a way it had not in the past; experiencing Rome less like tourists and more like friends and temporary residents in a city they would tour four more times in subsequent years. The meal finished with grappa and that, along with 'Gaffer', entered the tour vocabulary. The effects of the former would subside the following morning but the warmth towards Filippo and the 'Gaffer' would last, reciprocated by their pride in the team's performance on the pitch and their companionship, curiosity and good humour off it.

The following day, they made their way by a combination of metro, scooter and foot from their base in Hotel des Artistes, close to Termini station, for a tour of Rome's ancient sites, breaking off to pick up pieces of focaccia, a late coffee and an early *aperitivo*. They also had to plan that evening's entertainment as Filippo would be unable to join them due to family commitments. Various options were proposed but in the great traditions of British football teams abroad they went to – the opera.

Alan Johns, 'Cornish Al' as he was known to teammates, was described by Stefan Howald as a mercurial player on the pitch, capable of changing a game with a mazy dribble, a dangerous cross or an early shot. At other times and particularly if he was partnering Raj Chada in the centre of midfield, he could be slow to track back and reluctant to tackle. Off the pitch, he was also an unexpected entity. He was a proud Cornishman who had maintained his accent and retained a strong loyalty to the land of his origins. He had been a high flier at Magdalen College in Oxford, which led to a rapid rise as a barrister, moving ahead of others from more privileged backgrounds. Just before he joined PFFC he had undergone a religious conversion which brought some change to his lifestyle and outlook. His politics differed from the rest of the squad, most of whom were to varying degrees left of centre; Johns, by comparison, was of a more conservative disposition though shared the essential ethos of the club, notably its belief that football should be played for its simple pleasures without rancour, retribution or regular training sessions. Like several of the other players who joined after 2000, he could have played at a higher level but preferred to turn out for a like-minded group who enjoyed being together; he himself was a jovial and hospitable squad member who put a strong emphasis on team spirit. His party tricks included a rendition of Frank Sinatra's greatest hits and reciting poetry at end-of-year dinners. He also loved opera.

That evening, the squad minus Filippo (and Smithers, who was still to reappear from his mother's clutches) set off for St Paul's Within the Walls, an Anglican church on Via Nazionale, which was hosting a performance of Puccini's *La Boheme*. This was a first taste of live opera for most of the squad and it was a memorable one, partly for the quality of the voice of the leading lady – one prima donna deemed acceptable to an increasingly close-knit squad – and partly for the unexpected entertainment at each interval. This was provided by Dennis Skinner, a British member of parliament not previously known for exotic foreign travel or the attractions of high culture. Yet here was the 'Beast of Bolsover', accompanied by an American lady friend, as surprised to bump into a British football team in an Italian opera audience as they were to meet him. In three different helpings, Skinner reassured the squad that he had not travelled on parliamentary expenses, recounted his playing days at Ruskin College (where Andrews had also been a student), and proposed his own words of wisdom for a future Philosophy Football shirt, 'Football is about team-work and it's about fooking war.'

The evening concluded with a late-night disco on a boat on the Tiber, even if the dancing lacked the discipline imposed by the two banks of four the previous day. Boyle later summed up the moves of the key players.

Ian: Danced like Tony Adams: authoritative but often static

Owen: Steven Gerrard: good touch, great engine, never stopped

Rob: Robbie Savage: savage

Richard: Steve McManaman: flashes of sublime skill but flattered to deceive

Jez: Emmanuel Petit: classy and knew it
Raj: Mark Hughes: traces of a glorious past, but the pace got to him

The end of what was generally agreed to be a groundbreaking tour for team bonding ended on another high the following day when the squad went to the Stadio Olimpico to watch AS Roma beat Udinese. This was to be a title-winning season for Roma: could their early pace-setting be a good omen as PFFC returned to the Grafton Millennium League?

Unfortunately, after the heights of Rome, the team did not continue in similar vein when they got back to London. This was despite a well-earned draw against high-flying Strollers in a game which saw a promising debut from a new forward. Sola Akingbola, with his pace and dribbling ability, was providing much needed support for Stefan Howald, now nearing 50. Sola, who was born in Nigeria and moved to London with his family as a child, quickly fitted in to the formation and the ethos of the team and was only sorry he could not make the post-match drink because of 'band practice'. It was only a couple of months later, after a larger than usual crowd had gathered at Regent's Park to watch the team, that it transpired that his 'band' was Jamiroquai; he was its percussionist and 'band practice' was in fact preparation for the imminent release of their fifth album, *A Funk Odyssey*, preceded by a huge European tour. Ricci, who had seen the band live in Italy a couple of times in previous years, was stunned by the episode. 'So, you have a member of a world-famous band in your team and you don't know it?' he asked in astonishment. 'Okay, he's shy and you have privacy as the first commandment over here. And yes, possibly in Italy we tend to dive into other people's lives without many attentions, but still … I can't believe you didn't even ask who he is playing with. Out of curiosity, or politeness, or at least to show some kind of basic interest in what he's doing.'

The next match was a more disappointing 1-1 draw with lowly Falcon, played in atrocious conditions in Regent's Park. Filippo was not happy. The Gaffer was in Italy, beginning a new book about Italian politics. The team lacked shape and quality but worst of all, so far as Filippo was concerned, there was too much complacency and not enough fight. PFFC still had an outside chance of winning the league, and he took issue with the players' attitudes, which in his view were lacking the 'never say die' British values he had come to expect. Had their newly won 'Europeanness' – even stronger after a long weekend in Rome – made them a little too cosmopolitan, to the detriment of the competitive spirit needed to win football matches?

There followed a long dressing room rant in imperfect English that had been further adulterated by the preceding 90 minutes in the mud. To the stunned silence of his team-mates and the bemusement of the opponents with whom they had to share the dressing-room, he let loose:

'We entered the field with the disgraceful "easy game" attitude and wasted the first half. Where was the electricity, rage, or grit? Perhaps I'm a bit weird but I really feel bad when my team is not capable of win these games. To my personal opinion, and my personal fitness, the Grafton League is the Premier League.'

This was Filippo's 'hairdryer moment' to match Alex Ferguson's tirade against his young stars. In Filippo's case it evoked another culture clash and not only because he was then the only one of 250 Regent's Park regulars to possess a hairdryer, which required him to negotiate an arrangement with Phyllis, the custodian of the changing rooms, whose office contained the one and only socket. This was the beginning of a long rapport with 'Lady Phyllis', a strong character with southern Italian origins. Between them there was some mutual understanding of the peculiarities of the English.

The following day in his email Filippo apologised for the tone of his outburst, though not for its essential message. He had grown up in Rome in the 1970s and 1980s in awe of the fighting spirit of British football. 'We loved the atmosphere, the passion, the stamina, the rhythm, the shirts, the stadia, the colours, the chants, the grass, the mud of this *calcio inglese*.' To see such a reaction from his team was a disappointment, therefore. However, he hoped 'we can build on this incident', which of course followed the earlier culture clashes.

It seemed to pay off. In a late flurry of high-scoring matches PFFC responded with a 4-2 win in the return fixture with Falcon, thrashed champions-elect South Indies 5-1, with a hat-trick from Johns, lost 6-5 to Inter

Aztec after leading 3-0, and defeated Grafton 5-2 at their posh Dulwich College ground. This last match was another memorable one for Filippo as he scored his first goal for the club, an occasion which precipitated another chase, this time of a more joyful nature. The spectacle of a bare-chested Filippo waving his shirt at the traffic on the South Circular (followed by Matteo Patrono, over from Rome for the weekend) was enough to earn him a yellow card from the referee as well as the inaugural 'goal celebration of the year' award at the PFFC end-of-season party.

Reflecting on his first season, Filippo sought to explain its peculiarities as he found them, by publishing his 'Ten Commandants of English Football':

1: Referring to England as the home of grass football is the first mistake. Almost 50 per cent of our league games were played on astroturf. Something weird and unthinkable. And dangerous.

2: To play in England you have to learn a few words. Most of them are strictly related to the game, others have a vaguer connection. 'Waterlogged' is the term most in vogue throughout the winter. Even when it's not raining the pitches are declared waterlogged. This means a continuous earthquake in the league fixtures and can lead to undesirable trips to south London for nothing.

3: Another term that you should learn to use properly is the mythical 'unlucky'. Okay, we all know that technique is not the best weapon sent from God to English players. We also know the proverbial solidarity and group spirit that underpin English teams. But hearing a unanimous shout of 'unlucky!' from your team-mates when one of you has just shot at goal only for it to 'unluckily' end on the M3 (southbound) is truly hard to understand.

4: Also very popular is the word 'Gaffer'. Before joining the Grafton Millennium League I'd read this at the end of films. And being a writer of international standing, I've also heard it in French, where they refer to the *Gaffeur* as someone who makes gaffes. The link between those two identifications and football remains missing to me.

5: The last word I'll mention still remains an enigma to your author. I'm talking about 'Mallard'. I was awarded it at the AGM for the 'goal celebration of the year', but still the true meaning escapes me.

6: Then, the summer came. Okay, summer is perhaps too strong a concept for these latitudes, but they call it this. And, when they say summer, they also say it's cricket time. Coming from the continent, you think about cricket as a sport followed by ten octogenarians and played by some of their friends. How wrong. Pages and pages in the newspapers. As such, you can live with it, but it also means the transformation of all London's grass pitches, now available at last without being waterlogged, into cricket grounds.

7: In Italy we describe wild and truly lax refereeing as 'English refereeing'. Now I've experienced it on my delicate skin. Bloody hell! Contact, that in any other country around the world (except perhaps Nigeria, Colombia and Uruguay) would be sanctioned with a sacrosanct yellow card isn't even considered by the man in black. And don't dare to ask for a free kick.

8: Strictly related to the previous point is the voting scale used to judge the performances of the players. When it comes to defenders, the most relevant criterion is the number of tackles you've managed to sink into your opponents' ankles.

From there, and only from there, other evaluations will be possibly taken into account.

9: The dressing room policy is also something you have to be aware of. Nothing can be left inside because it seems England is a kind of giant colosseum: no keys and too many doors. Then, if you're planning to enter the dressing rooms with all the accessories that make up normal kit for us European footballers, be prepared to be called: a) weirdo; b) poof; c) French; d) posh.

The four terms could even be applied at the same time. And this, simply because you have placed in your bag:

a) Flip-flops to keep your feet clean when manoeuvring over a five-inch high mud barrier that separates your bench from the shower.

b) Bath robe to dry yourself with something larger than the highly popular beer towel which to me seems a bit small for six-foot-tall men. Then, also having another small towel which you reserve for your head drives them crazy. What a waste! If you want to do as the English do, then be prepared to get dry with a beer towel that you've also used to take away the mud from your feet. Before or after using it on the rest of your body is left to your discretion.

c) Shower gel and shampoo, which seem to mean to the lads that you're incredibly rich. Another inadmissible waste of money. One product is more than enough, and in fact many players just use water.

d) Hairdryer, the mother of all insults to a true Sunday League footballer. No further comments are needed, apart from the fact that when I asked the lady who governs the Regent's Park dressing rooms for a plug for my hairdryer she stared at me and said (with an unmistakeable Italian-

Corleonese accent), 'You're not English, are you?' Life needs certainties.

10: The beer after the game is something you can't renounce. Dead or alive, or, more accurately, shower or no shower. If you play football, then you have to go to the pub. And if 'unluckily' you couldn't use the shower after a 90-minute battle on a rainy day on a muddy pitch, the lads down at the local boozer will definitely understand you. And won't even look at your poor state. Football is a universal language. We are at the pub and the game's over. Here, the last recommendation: don't dare to order any food that doesn't belong to the crisp family. 'Come on, you bloody European, you aren't thinking of eating something after a two-hour drive to south London, a 90-minute game with no subs and before you drink a couple of pints with nothing to fill your stomach since that curry you had last night on the way home. Are you?'

Filippo had learnt the British lessons of football. Equally importantly, his team-mates had adopted the European mentality that was triggered in Zurich, harnessed in Rome and adapted with the help of their Italian talisman in London. What could this bring to their fortunes on the pitch?

4

Prague, Pordenone and Parisot

THE 2000/01 season had ended on a high with the 5-1 thrashing of the champions South Indies a late highlight. Buoyed by a surge of good results and with Filippo's dressing room outburst still ringing in their ears, the team was now more confident and expected to win (or at least avoid defeat) every time they took the pitch. This was in sharp contrast to its earlier history, when coming away with an 'unlucky' 7-3 defeat was the basis for an optimistic match report which suggested hopeful signs were around the corner.

European travel had been the key factor in the reversal of fortunes, but the next overseas fixture was a reminder of darker times. Born from the ashes of the small British Communist Party in the aftermath of the fall of the Soviet system, a PFFC trip to Prague was an intriguing prospect. What would they find? How would PFFC's new-found international language of fraternity fare in the rebuilding of civil society (and its football associations) of the still new Czech Republic? How would the new generation of Czechs, saturated with the excesses of the major western European football leagues, find this alternative, anti-capitalist London team?

In fact, alongside the signs of a new society, they found that some remnants of the old system continued to be an obstacle for change. In extremely cold March temperatures, a depleted PFFC squad arrived for a match against a left-wing village workers' side. They had been invited by Miroslav, a former official of Czechoslovakia's football federation who was finding the transition from 'real socialism' to 'real capitalism' somewhat challenging. He still asserted some privileges, however. This included commandeering a regular city bus midway through its intended route to transport PFFC to the ground in time for kick-off. This was helped by the exchange of substantial koruna notes with the driver (to the bemusement of the passengers on board), so that the team could be delivered on time to Zlatníky-Hodkovice, a small village located in deepest Bohemia.

In 1967, at one of the pivotal moments in the history of Scottish football, Celtic arrived in the same city for their second-leg semi-final against Dukla Prague, an army-based team and the less-well known of the Prague clubs. Celtic led 3-1 from the first leg in Glasgow, and with a solid defensive formation and in an icy wind, the 'Iron Curtain Celts' (as one newspaper reported it) held out against their Czech opponents. Over the two legs, it was the pace of the Scottish forwards and the tenacity of their defending that took them through to the final and the later glory of being European champions.

For some of the Liverpool-supporting PFFC players who had been brought up on the edgy, satirical music of the post-punk era, Celtic's defeated opponents resonated for different reasons. In 'All I Want for Christmas is a Dukla Prague Away Kit', the Birkenhead band Half Man Half Biscuit, founded by a former editor of a football fanzine, lamented the failings of a Subbuteo team whose impressive strip was not matched by results on the pitch. That would be the case with PFFC on this tour.

Hugh Tisdale, the designer of the Philosophy Football shirts and co-founder of the company, was a major (non-playing) addition to the Prague tour party; by the end of that season he would be a familiar figure next to the Gaffer on the touchline, cheering the team on with his large 1950s-style rattle. Tisdale ensured they were kitted out in new strips with a barcoded design, a suitable satire on corporate power and the rejection of sponsorship logos. Over the next few years, PFFC's players would be afforded a regular supply of pristine, beautifully crafted words of dissent, commemoration and enlightenment. Occasionally, performances on the pitch did justice to the shirts. This was not one of those occasions.

On arrival, they found their opponents were a young, fit and organised local team who played together every week. By contrast the PFFC line-up that took to the pitch was more reminiscent of its earlier days and Andrews was grateful to two former players, journalists (and QPR-supporting friends) Ivor Gaber and Christian Wolmar, who had been recruited at the last minute. The depleted squad also included two employees of the British Embassy in Prague, neither of whom provided any evidence that they had previously kicked a football.

Matters on the pitch had not been helped by an injury to tour captain Ian Coyne, who strained his neck in an impromptu training session carried out in arctic conditions two days before. At least Miroslav was able to use some influence to get him prompt attention at the local clinic. The match ended in a 7-0 thrashing. Showers, even colder than those in Regent's Park in January, greeted the losing philosophers before a dinner of hranolky (chips) at the village clubhouse where the culinary offerings revived memories of pre-1989 eastern Europe.

Perhaps the highlight of the trip was a visit on the final day to watch a match between Viktoria Žižkov and Brno, which poignantly recalled PFFC's founding commitment to celebrate the simple pleasures of football. Standing on the terraces and enjoying cheap food and drink, PFFC discovered that the costs of a season ticket for the home team here was equivalent to the price of a glossy replica shirt of a famous European player on sale in the centre of Prague. It was certainly more absorbing as a spectacle than the World Cup qualifier between Czech Republic and Denmark they had seen at the start of the tour – a 0-0 stalemate. The squad were bored enough to attempt a dialogue with Graham Poll, the English referee officiating. On the last day Miroslav, the host, organiser, benefactor, and chief negotiator was nowhere to be seen. He had promised to take the team on a tour of the local brewery, but either PFFC had not lived up to his expectations or he did not relish being faced with more proof of his waning influence.

Prague was one of four trips PFFC made to the fast-changing Europe in the course of nine months. Zurich and Rome had created a thirst for more and the low-cost airlines facilitated an unlikely end-of-season visit to Pordenone in the Friuli Venezia Giulia region in north-eastern Italy. In the post-war period it had been one of the military towns used as a potential fortress against possible Soviet invasion. Now, like the rest of Italy, it was embroiled in the early stages of the populist politics that would sweep Europe over the next 15 years. The rise in support for Silvio Berlusconi was partly a response to the end of the Cold War and the collapse of the Christian Democrats and Communists in the wake of corruption scandals and the fall of the Berlin Wall. PFFC had been invited to take part in a five-a-side tournament during the local election campaign by Mick Walton, an exiled English language teacher who was a candidate on the civic list (a group of independent candidates).

Here, Soviet communists were no longer a threat and the main points of contention among an enormous variety of candidates and parties, whose array of political ideas were incomprehensible even to the more politically informed philosophers, were largely confined to personal characteristics and local standing. This was despite the fact that Walton's civic list, known as Fiume (river), was in a tight three-sided battle against the alliance of Silvio Berlusconi's Forza Italia, the post-fascist National Alliance and the regionalist (and xenophobic) Northern League, and (as the third strand), the centrist Margherita ('Daisy') group.

Walton, a passionate Sheffield United supporter, had heard about PFFC and wanted to add something a bit different to the normal patterns of Italian provincial politics, and calculated that football would be an effective medium through which to appeal to the electorate in Italy. PFFC made a small impact which reached the local paper, though this had less to do with their performance in the tournament and more to do with the unlikely spectacle of a British amateur team turning up in the middle of an Italian election campaign. At least they were dressed appropriately, Tisdale having designed a splendid Niccolò Machiavelli shirt bearing the words 'Each succeeds in reaching the goal by a different method', which seemed to be an ideal accompaniment to the complex procedures required to win a majority in a local Italian election. Indeed, while PFFC did not win the tournament, Sergio Bolzonello, the centre-left candidate, was elected mayor of Pordenone on Walton's list.

Walton would be involved in the club's subsequent trips dedicated to Pier Paolo Pasolini, poet, film director and, at the end of his life, scourge of Italy's political elite, who lived (and played football) in the Friuli Venezia region. Pasolini and Machiavelli, two Italian philosophers who understood the mechanisms of power, would regularly feature as PFFC's away strips. The following year Walton took part in one of PFFC's occasional political events. Despite its robust founding principles politics had been less of a priority in recent times, but their combative midfielder and player of the season, Raj Chada, a Labour Party activist, had decided to stand for election to Camden Council. As Walton had done in Pordenone, Chada organised a football tournament as part of his campaign. Football in the Communities was held at the Malden Road pitches, in the middle of a housing estate. From Italy, Walton brought his own team, Socially Useful Football Team, and other men's and women's teams represented different Camden communities. The men's tournament was won by a Somalian team, and the women's trophy taken by a group of solicitors nicknamed the Bluebells which featured Tracey Crouch, a future minister for sport in the Conservative government. PFFC defeated the local Labour Party in a hard-fought fixture, but Labour – and Chada – were elected at the polls.

Shortly after Pordenone, Andrews would know more about the exercise of power in Berlusconi's Italy when he went to report on the G8 summit protests in Genoa. There he found the centre of the city controlled by red and yellow zones and running clashes between demonstrators and police which continued over a weekend of violence and culminated with the death of a young demonstrator, Carlo Giuliani, who was shot dead by a policeman. The violent raid on the Armando Diaz school led to international protests, a condemnation by the European Court of Human Rights and a film, 'Diaz – Don't clean up this blood'. Among the counter-cultural alternative summit he came across more peaceful anarchism, including Pink Silver marchers promising 'tactical frivolity', and an intriguing banner proclaiming 'Slow Food', held by a group in Lucca, Tuscany.

CAYLUS, PARISOT, PUYLAGARDE
Tournoi de football
pour une philosophie d'ouverture

If European politics provided a stormier, less predictable backstory to a 'left-wing football team', then its cultural benefits continued to inspire the squad, as they discovered in a sedate week-long pre-season trip to the south of France. Hugh Tisdale's involvement with the club had enabled a smoother process of selecting and distributing the different Philosophy Football strips worn by the players, some of which would be specially commissioned and designed for the tours. On meeting them he was impressed by the close camaraderie of the squad, which he found to be 'rich in character and united in a belief that football is a game to be savoured for its simple beauty'. They reciprocated the affection, quickly dubbing him 'The Chairman'. Tisdale now offered the hospitality of his holiday home in Carcassonne, in advance of a tournament with like-minded teams in the village of Parisot, Tarn-et-Garonne in south-eastern France. It was a big effort on the part of Tisdale and his partner Deborah; in addition to the regular squad of PFFC players he also accommodated a makeshift PFFC women's team, largely made up of the players' partners, who would feature in the women's tournament.

After a welcoming party at his old farmhouse, where the local wine, Blanquette de Limoux, flowed freely, the large squad set off on a four-hour drive early the next morning for a packed programme of two full match friendlies against local village teams, followed by a day-long *tournoi*. Proceedings started inauspiciously with a 4-1 drubbing at the hands of the local team Entente Sportive Parisot Puylagarde, but the following day brought a change in luck – and atmosphere – among the squad. Following a creditable 0-0 draw between the PFFC's ad hoc women's team and local opponents, PFFC's evening match against Caylus, the neighbouring village, kicked off at precisely the moment that the England national team started their crucial World Cup qualifier against Germany in Munich. Filippo, at home in Maida Vale, west London, but with an ear on events in France, was following what would be a historic victory. As England's unlikely 5-1 hammering of their long-standing rivals took shape, he sent updated text messages to the Gaffer, who was on the touchline in Caylus waiting to make another brief post-retirement cameo at left-back. The Caylus match, however, was played in failing light as the early autumn nights closed in and although it brought an improved performance, was no match for the drama in Munich. As the England goals went in and PFFC's game drifted towards a worthy goalless draw in the darkness, the contrasting scenes were recaptured in the match report, which merged Filippo's 'real-time' texts with the Gaffer's summary of the Caylus conundrum.

Min 6: 'Jancker 1-0, defence slept' / Floodlights flicker on and off in Caylus, but no snoring in Philosophy's defence as skipper Kayley marshals troops to thwart first attack by home side. Already early signs of greater philosophical endeavour than the night before as the visitors get to grips with dodgy pitch.

Min 13: 'Michael Owen, who else? 1-1' / Crunching tackle in the twilight zone. Owen Mather, who else?

First half injury time: 'Long range, Gerrard, 2-1 England' / End of shortened first half due to floodlight failure, Cornish Al, in on goal hits inside of post. It was to be the Thinkers' best chance all night.

Min 48: 'First international double for Owen. England 3-1' / Another floodlight goes as Gaffer comes on at left-back and relies on Owen for double vision.

Min 66: 'What about a third by Owen? England 4 Germany 1. In Munich' / What about a sight of Owen? Squinting Gaffer trying to take throw-in. In total darkness.

Min 74: 'Can U believe it? Scholes to Heskey 5-1' / Can you see it? Ian attempts ambitious overhead kick. Apparently. Gets injured in the process. Gaffer appeals against the light.

PFFC's players will always remember where they were the night England beat Germany 5-1. As so often with English football this proved to another false dawn rather than renaissance but to a group of mainly English players on tour in France it brought a vital boost in confidence which was carried into the following day's *tournoi*. Once again PFFC took on Parisot Puylagarde, their opponents of two days before, as well as two other teams, Najac and Verfeil. In good spirits, they managed to persuade the organisers to blast out The Specials' 'Enjoy Yourself' each time they took the field, which won some sympathy and a little bemusement from the locals. Inspired performances followed, and, led by Alan Johns – '*superbe*', according to an onlooker – they won the trophy, with two wins and two draws.

The end-of-tour meal, consisting in the main of the inner parts of duck and chicken cooked by local farmers, was another new experience and another sign of European conviviality on tour – in contrast to the more austere conditions and indifferent relations between league rivals in London.

Speeches and pleasantries were exchanged with the help of Claire Gorrara, lecturer in French (and Boyle's partner) and PFFC's growing taste and appreciation of what Europe had to offer was reflected in the Gaffer's post-tournament interview with local paper *La Depeche du Midi*, where he described France as being 'at the heart of modern philosophy, the centre of football excellence [they were World Cup holders at the time] and the home of good food'.

Philosophy football en finale du tournoi franco-anglais

In a hectic tour schedule, Prague, Pordenone and Parisot had provided further injections of European culture and plenty of experiences to savour and to reflect upon after they returned. Meanwhile Filippo, whose commitments for his newspaper and as a pundit on *Football Italia* had kept him in London during the year, was continuing to adapt to British culture. He had been born in Reggio Emilia, a small city in the north of Italy, and had grown up in Rome. But deep down he often thought of London as his new city, an emotional attachment that was cemented through the experiences and stories of his five older brothers who had been travelling to London since the early 1970s, for the music, the arts and the style.

As the Riccis were a football family too – Filippo's father became a sports journalist after starting as a teacher – he, like other Italians, was easily caught up in the passion for English football. He adopted Liverpool as his 'foreign' team in playground matches at school, while the fortunes of English teams featured regularly on TeleRoma 56, after Michele Plastino, a broadcast journalist and pioneering promoter of televised sport, managed to capture the rights to screen matches from the former English First Division in a deal that would be unimaginable in the era of the Premier League. Therefore, along with other Italians, Filippo had a glimpse of English football, which was then dominant in Europe. He loved everything: the passion, the grit, the physical nature, the attitude, the pace (even the violence) on and off the pitch. Compared to the tactical niceties of Italian football and its enduring love for the theatrical and the artistic (while tolerating cheating as an acceptable route to victory), it was the more ruthless nature of English football that inspired him.

His first visit to London was in the summer of 1983, arriving by train via Paris. He immediately fell in love with the city. The smell of fish and chips, and the unmistakable atmosphere of the Tube would stay with him forever, implanting memories that would remain vivid in later years.

He slept in a hostel in Holland Park, was pickpocketed in a Kings Road pub and on the third night went to The Heaven to attend a memorable gay night at that club situated under the arches of Charing Cross Station. Here he encountered Marc Almond and Boy George, Sade and Jimmy Somerville, enormous skinheads with swastikas on their t-shirts, kissing themselves on the dance floor, and the best music he had ever heard.

Coming from the eternal but in many ways very provincial Rome, this was a revolutionary awakening: mind-blowing, upsetting and unbelievable. The freedoms, the openness, the transgression, the modernity all palpable in London where they had been absent at home. The city was enormous but became immediately so familiar. He bought his first pair of Doc Marten's in a Camden Town shoe shop for £20. London was cheap at the time. And dirty, and wild. He was fascinated. He bought his first England football shirt in a shop in Elephant and Castle, and a first pair of 'loafers' at Robot in Covent Garden.

Filippo became a regular at the Exchange record shops, while buying clothes on daily excursions to the Kings Road (already fashionable and expensive). He came for the music which at that time he loved even more than the football. But it was while dancing with Leigh Bowery at the Taboo in Leicester Square and befriending Mark Moore and Philip Sallon (at the time, the former was a DJ while the latter was the main character at the Mud Club in Charing Cross Road), he became a regular at the beloved Sportspages bookshop on the same road. In Italy, football literature was extremely limited, but in London he had found heaven.

For four consecutive summers he travelled from Rome to London, enjoying the explosion of the house music and then the summer of love. But football was always on his mind. He couldn't play in London because he had been clubbing all night and waking up late. He didn't bring boots and as a proper fashion victim did not want to ruin his stylish haircut. However, his appointment with the *calcio inglese* that he loved so much was only delayed indefinitely.

Seventeen years after his first visit to London football had overruled music in the order of priorities. By September 2000 he was now making a living as a sports journalist. He still went clubbing with his wife (whom he met on a dance floor) but more in the evening than at night, as regulars at Lazy Dog, run by Ben Watt of Everything but the Girl in Notting Hill, which they attended on weekday afternoons after working in different London stadia covering Premier League matches. Once again, London surprised him. The city had changed. It was much more cosmopolitan, ('full of bloody foreigners'), with glasses of wine beginning to threaten the dominance of the pint. But London's spirit was still there, forcing people coming from abroad to adapt and creating in the process a very interesting blend. Professionally, Filippo and Benedetta (a football photographer) found London to be a land of opportunities, as it was for many others who came from abroad, or from other parts of the UK. They felt and experienced the same. London was growing. It was hard, sometimes extremely hard and even unpleasant, before even getting on to the weather. But if you were determined enough you could survive and progress. This was the new London: rigid, full of rules, cold and wet, but also wonderful and open.

Shortly after arriving in London, Filippo contacted the production company behind *Football Italia*, the programme that covered Italian football in the UK and was hosted by James Richardson. Before long he found himself next to Richardson, utilising his Italian accent live on Channel 4 for the benefit of British TV viewers now fascinated by the football of his country. He felt he was giving something back. Impressed by Richardson's professionalism, he was also intrigued by this amiable, humorous Englishman's passion for Italy. On TV his gestures were appreciated, and he began to exchange opinions and ideas on the state of Italian football with a young journalist called Gab Marcotti as well as some of the former players who had spent some time in Italy. Among them were the late Ray Wilkins, Joe Jordan, Paul Elliott, David Platt, Liam Brady, Trevor Francis, Tony Dorigo and the legendary Luther Blissett. Occasionally, he was alongside his compatriot Roberto Di Matteo. He was a pundit, and becoming quite popular in England, while relatively unknown in his native Italy.

In fact, a reverse scenario in Italy whereby an unknown English journalist would be welcomed with open arms after knocking on the door of an Italian TV station was unimaginable. Filippo had had a similar (and for him, an astonishing) experience when covering African football in 1993. He got in touch with the BBC World Service and started to collaborate with them, soon invited to the famous Bush House to do a training course as he had never worked in radio before. The 'Beeb', in Italy (as elsewhere in the world), was still revered and respected.

Emboldened by his access to the British media, he started contributing to *The Observer*, while Benedetta, as a new, young and female football photographer, benefited from the same openness of British journalism. Her pictures were sent to all the leading newspapers and despite them having their own photographers at the same game (and paying the powerful international agencies), if they liked her shots they used them and paid generously, both of which would have been impossible in Italy, where nepotism and poor rewards were common.

Just a year after arriving from Italy, Filippo felt fully embraced by his new country. He was watching an enormous amount of Premier League matches and was playing Sunday football. As a journalist, Stamford Bridge was his 'home' pitch because it had effectively become an 'Italian' club. Gianluca Vialli, Claudio Ranieri, Gianfranco Zola, Roberto Di Matteo, Carlo Cudicini and Sam Dalla Bona were only a few of the names that built a strong link between the Blues and the Azzurri. And Chelsea epitomised the change in British football culture. In one of his articles Filippo described how Ken Bates sold the club to Roman Abramovich for £1, and then in another about how the Russian oligarch started a spending spree that continues to this day. Arsène Wenger, Eric Cantona, David Ginola, Zola, Dennis Bergkamp, José Mourinho, Rafa Benitez, Thierry Henry, Robert Pires, Cristiano Ronaldo and all the other foreigners changed English football for good. The fact that no English manager has won the Premier League since

the competition changed its name is also symbolic of the transformation that was already under way before Filippo arrived.

But while writing about the radical changes sustained by the elite in English football, Filippo, through PFFC, was able to measure the changes alongside the grassroots experiences he encountered in the Sunday competitions. It would always be a sharp contrast that he treasured in his London years. He knew that what he was witnessing as a player had been somehow 'betrayed' by the Premier League, at the time focused only on becoming a global business. The romanticism, the ugliness, the rough play, the spirit of the game, also included, on a Sunday, its most comical, sometimes ridiculous, sometimes cute aspects. These were still alive and kicking in Regent's Park.

From the outset he felt torn, because he knew he was contributing to PFFC's transformation (which meant dispensing with some of the attributes he admired as a boy) by introducing some food into the liquid post-game routine, or wine, or flip-flops. Occasionally he wondered if he was poisoning the sanctity of English football with his hairdryer. At the same time, he was annoyed by the direction that the Premier League was heading: the prices, the tourists, the distance from the fans, the superhero tag applied to everyone and everything. Yet he ended up enjoying both 'footballs': the one he was playing, as well as the one he was watching and reporting on. Above all, he continued to enjoy London.

5

A Winning Formula: Football Meets Philosophy

NEW RECRUITS continued to come in from all over London, and from different walks of life. The addition of Neil James, a prolific forward who had represented New Zealand schoolboys but had played more rugby since arriving in London in 1990, turned out to be crucial to the team's improvement over the next couple of seasons. James was introduced to the team by Brian Bannister, a Liverpool-supporting public relations consultant, who after a brief appearance the previous season was now the regular centre-back partner for Evertonian Paul Kayley. At well over 6ft 6in he would later be described as the 'biggest defender in the world' by a BBC opponent. This strengthened the squad, providing cover in all positions, and after the encouraging end to the previous season there was a new confidence in the team.

This was confirmed by early results, with James's debut goal bringing victory against Grafton; another narrow victory by the same 1-0 score over Inter Aztec and two 7-2 thrashings, firstly of Falcon (with three goals from Stefan Howald), and the return match with Grafton, in which Ian Coyne, now enjoying a central midfield role, also scored a hat-trick. In between, they lost a dramatic cup tie against Cameron Athan, a boys' club from Walthamstow with a 70-year history, and whose former players included Teddy Sheringham, while David Beckham started his career for one of their league opponents, Ridgeway Rovers. They normally played at a much higher level in the Essex Senior League, but in the torrential downpour at Regent's Park, with Brian Bannister (later compared by his team-mates to a great whale) defying all opposition attacks in the mud and the rain in an outstanding individual performance the game went into extra time with PFFC eventually succumbing 4-2.

Results continued to improve. It was a stronger squad, but the key to PFFC's rising success was another European addition. Marco Capecelatro was an old friend of Filippo who had recently left Rome for London in search of work. A part-time musician, his other passion was football and after warning him of the peculiarities of the English game, Filippo brought him to PFFC: his first of several Italian signings. A naturally gifted and elegant footballer, Capecelatro, like his old friend, found it difficult at first to adjust to the culture shock that confronted him every Sunday morning, as long balls were sent over his head to utilise the pace of Stefan Howald. He despaired at the lack of composure and pleaded with his team-mates for short passes 'to feet'.

It was clear that Capecelatro's arrival in the team meant a new formation had to be considered; one which would draw on his strengths. Normally PFFC had gone with the familiar 4-4-2 and occasionally 4-5-1. But Marco was a classic number ten and to get the best out of him they needed to give him the role which allowed him to dictate the play. At the same time, the Gaffer and Filippo knew that Howald was at his best playing off another striker. Therefore, they came up with a 4-3-1-2 system, a version of what would later become normalised in British football as the 'diamond', in which a narrow formation in midfield would be compensated by full-backs quickly getting forward on the flanks. This was the theory anyway and initially it brought great dividends by unsettling opponents who were not used to picking up a floating, skilful Italian who was looking to take the ball in a deep position or make late runs into the penalty box.

Success on the pitch relieved some of the organisational burden. The Gaffer found that it was always easier to get a full squad out when the team was winning. It was a long-standing joke that kick-off times were never revealed and that everyone had to be at the ground at 9.45am to avoid any uncertainty generated by late arrivals. Organisation was key, as was the time to prepare and talk through the match in advance, with Filippo and the Gaffer now engaged in prolonged conversations about this or that player or formation. Home fixtures at Regent's Park were easiest to arrange. On the other hand, away matches in remote parts of south London, on the Surrey borders, meant players were required to travel in mini car convoys. Filippo would pick up the Gaffer somewhere in Westminster, stopping off at Waterloo to meet Owen Mather and anyone else who needed a lift.

This almost military-style precision unfortunately fell away at the most decisive point in the season. Along with PFFC, Inter Aztec were making the early running at the top of the Grafton Millennium League. Over the next two seasons these two teams would battle it out in closely and often controversial contests and the results of the two fixtures effectively decided the league, in the way that Celtic and Rangers jostled for the Scottish Premier League. The previous year, Inter Aztec had beaten PFFC 6-5 in an end-of-season fixture which had no significance for the league, except as a precursor of the closely fought battles to come. At the end of February PFFC made the long journey to Hampton Court for a crucial away fixture between the two top teams. PFFC had won their home match 1-0 back in November, so Aztec needed to win on their own patch to restore parity. They had strong ambitions to win the league and PFFC were the main obstacle.

For once, PFFC's formidable organisation was lacking. The venue seemed to have been omitted from the London

A-Z and Google Maps was a long way off. In those days mobile phones sent text messages or, if you had a good enough reception, an urgent phone call. Three players arrived late and Ian Coyne five minutes after the match had begun. This left the Gaffer more stressed than usual and with Filippo injured, they had to come up with a revised plan. Out went 4-3-1-2 and in, for the first time, was a back three, partly to counter Aztec's free-scoring (and very young) striker. It was a disaster. By the time Coyne had arrived PFFC were already losing, with full-backs unable to adapt to unfamiliar centre-back territory and a general confusion amplified by what seemed contradictory advice emanating from Filippo and the Gaffer on the touchline. After 15 minutes they were 3-0 down and the Grafton League was slipping away.

At this point, the Gaffer and Filippo opted to revert to 4-3-1-2 and the new unity on the touchline was reflected on the pitch as PFFC edged their way back into the match. Coyne, the late arrival, was now imposing his 6ft 2in frame in the centre of midfield, mindful perhaps of not further incurring the wrath of the manager. A storming header from Bannister reduced the arrears and then Mather, in his advancing left-back role – crucial to the formation – was urged by Filippo, inches away from him on the touchline, to continue a late run into the box which resulted in his first (and only) PFFC goal. It was 3-2, and then an extraordinary first half was concluded with Neil James's equaliser. The match had turned.

With both sides only too aware of the importance of the game, tempers frayed and tackles were late. The tackle that got Big Brian Bannister into the referee's notebook was 'so late it was practically Chaucerian', Joe Boyle noted later. James's second goal put them ahead and, after Aztec equalised with a penalty, PFFC went in front again with a goal from Stefan Howald. The man of the match, however, was Marco Capecelatro who, after PFFC's shaky start, ran the show. The opposition could not cope with his movement and, situating himself just behind the two in-form strikers, he was able to carve out opportunities at will as the match progressed. Appropriately, he was at the centre of the last act of the drama. Losing 5-4, Inter Aztec went deep in PFFC territory in search of the equaliser against a resolute and packed defence; Capecelatro, by now shielding an injured shoulder, was the one outlet, and, picking up the ball following a clearance, he took the opponents on a merry chase first to the wing and then cutting inside towards goal before, in an attempted tackle, an Aztec defender diverted the ball past his own goalkeeper to make it 6-4. The defender's name, or at least nickname, was 'Butch Shakespeare'. It was a poignant reminder of PFFC's most dramatic game to date, epitomised in Joe Boyle's match report, which he recounted in appropriate Shakespearian acts ('A Comedy of Errors', 'The Taming of the Shrew', 'Measure for Measure' and 'All's Well That Ends Well'). 'Under the shadow of Hampton Court,' he concluded, 'we had to endure moments of tragedy, then comedy, before emerging with a result that would have historical implications.'

It was the turning point and PFFC were unbeaten for the remainder of the season. The match which would confirm they had won their first title had been moved because of a late fixture pile-up from the normal Sunday morning time to a Thursday evening kick-off under floodlights at Crystal Palace's National Sports Centre. The time of the match added to the drama. PFFC raced into a quick three-goal lead with Neil James, who had scored hat-tricks in the two previous games, notching another couple here before a fightback ensured a tense finish. Finally, the referee called time for a 5-2 victory and the title was greeted by some jubilation on the pitch; a particularly happy moment for those like Stefan Howald and captain Paul Kayley who could remember darker days.

For a team that now considered itself European – and a long time before 'Brexit' was even heard of – a match in Brussels was always on the cards. That prospect increased once Jez Bray, part of the class of 2000, had been seconded to work for the European Commission as an expert to research transmissible spongiform encephalopathies. Shortly after he arrived, Bray started turning out for one of the six European Commission teams in the Interbanque League and arranged an early season friendly for PFFC against the European Commission All-Stars, comprised of a mix of players from their six teams and captained by agriculture expert Dario Di Benedetto. Helpfully, through European Commission contacts, he also made a couple of late signings for PFFC to complete the squad.

Once again Hugh Tisdale designed special shirts for the occasion, marked with the tour's motto 'Culture is Currency', the brainchild of Goober Fox, now retired from playing, who looked after the team's website and contributed on cultural matters. Fox's idea, which reflected the club's values, was that the European Union should be seen not merely as an economic union but a place where culture should be given equal status. Thus, in the pre-Brexit days, PFFC had nailed its colours firmly to the mast of European unity. As they joined their opponents at the pre-match dinner at the restaurant In't Spinnekopke ('in the spider's web'), the talk among the Londoners, as they sat down to *moules marinières* and *frites*, was only of greater integration.

The tour saw the debut of Ally Clow, a Scottish 22-year-old part-time musician who had moved to London the previous autumn. Clow had spent some months editing highlights for Football League websites before his flat-mate Bruce Oxley, who would later play for PFFC, passed him a Philosophy Football advert for players. After a summer five-a-side tournament in south London, Clow's first proper match was therefore on the plush Brussels surface, at Le Centre Interinstitutionnel Europeen (CIE) at Overijse. It was a perfect debut as Clow, a pacy and skilful midfielder with youth on his side, scored twice in a 3-0 win. It was the beginning of a long career with PFFC; on and off the pitch, in a variety of roles, Clow would emerge as a protégé of the management team.

By a quirk of the fixture list, PFFC's defence of the Grafton League started with an away fixture at Inter Aztec, the scene of the key battle of the previous season. In *Football Against the Enemy* Simon Kuper describes the tense rivalries between Germany and Holland, Barcelona and Real Madrid and Celtic and Rangers among many others, but none of those had to rise at dawn to do battle with the Sunday morning B&Q traffic and get to the ground before breakfast was finished in order to play their grudge match under the shadow of Hampton Court, where Henry VIII planned the downfall and execution of his wives. This match was as dramatic as the last.

On this occasion the whole PFFC squad found their way to Hampton Court on time, with Inter Aztec this time starting a man short. In Aztec's pre-match programme – a friendly gesture to offer some calm before the storm closing PFFC were referred to as their 'bogey team', a phrase which irked captain Paul Kayley, who had twice led his team to victory over them in the previous season. Tension was already in the air when the teams kicked off. PFFC took an early lead when a shot from Clow was parried by the goalkeeper on to the bar only for Neil James to knock in the rebound. Clow, following his exploits in Brussels, now marked his league debut in similar fashion with a neat drive into the corner. Aztec fought back though and were causing trouble down the flanks. Mather, PFFC's regular left-back – along with Kayley the only ever-present in the title-winning season – was booked for a late tackle which brought more pushing and shoving. Another late tackle soon afterwards saw a second yellow for Mather, while the Aztec defender's retaliation brought a straight red card for his trouble. Mather, on his long walk off the pitch, did not exchange any glances with the Gaffer (though Filippo, taking pity on the young full-back and thinking as always of the result, was able to console him, 'Don't worry Owen, we've lost a full-back and they've lost their best player.')

By getting their own player sent off Aztec had relinquished any immediate advantage. They did pull one back early in the second half and in a hectic climax nearly grabbed a point, with the game ending in a 3-2 win for PFFC, though not before Filippo, playing in central defence alongside Kayley, picked up two yellow cards in further altercations, leaving PFFC to hold out with nine men. 'Philosophical it wasn't. Oh, what sweet memories came into mind of the refined match we had played days earlier in the leafy suburbs of Brussels!' commented Howald in his match report.

The next match, at home at Regent's Park, was a completely different affair. Neil James, who had scored ten goals in his last four league games since the end of the previous season, now notched up eight in a one-sided outing against Falcon which ended with a 17-1 victory for the home side. In its early years, PFFC had become accustomed to heavy defeats and this was confirmation of the progress that had been made. In addition to James's eight, there was another hat-trick for Ian Coyne and a debut goal for Zsolt Tomori, a new Hungarian player who came on as a second-half substitute.

Tomori had joined the team with the help of his sister, who was a work colleague of Marco Fontana, the second of the four Marcos to appear for the club (and thereafter known as 'Marco 2'). Tomori had played at a semi-professional level in his home country and on Saturdays turned out for a Ryman League side. His levels of fitness and technical ability stunned the Gaffer, while he became a popular figure among team-mates who promptly nicknamed him 'Puskas'. He was given a PF shirt with a quote from the iconic Hungarian player who had been part of the great team that had so mesmerised England in the famous 6-3 victory in 'The Match of the Century' at Wembley in 1953. There was one problem with PFFC's own Puskas. He did not speak any English. Each week his sister would receive the Gaffer's email about the forthcoming match and venue and would translate the arrangements to her brother. This made tactical team talks more of a challenge than usual.

PFFC's progress seemed irreversible but a pre-Christmas blip plunged the team into a mini crisis following an unexpected defeat to Grafton. Filippo had a long-term injury and the Gaffer was absorbed by political developments in Italy, following the growing demonstrations against Silvio Berlusconi's government. The problems culminated in the Grafton game and were compounded by the absence of several key players (including Neil James and Raj Chada, who missed most of the season through illness, and Marco 1 who had returned to Rome) and an injury in the first 15 minutes to Rob Adams. The 4-2 defeat was a wake-up call and produced an introspective email discussion and, from beneath the porticoes of Bologna, a strong missive from the Gaffer.

'Yesterday was waiting to happen. All season we have had trouble getting a team out … We have to ask why we need a squad that is twice as large as any other team in the league and bigger than most in the Premiership … We still have an excellent chance of winning this league if we win our remaining matches. In order to do it, we need to have 14 players at EVERY match … Remember: we are the champions and we are defending our title. We now need to regroup and stand together more and fight for the cause.'

Knowing they had to win all their remaining matches to be sure of winning the league, the Christmas crisis was followed by a marked upturn in form and results. PFFC won ten successive games (another record), including a 4-0 drubbing of Inter Aztec, to hold on to their title. They had responded to the Gaffer's call at Christmas and once again found consistency in performance and depth in the squad. But they would not have won the league without the extraordinary goalscoring feats of Neil James, who netted 40 times in 13 matches, which won him both the Grafton League's Golden Boot and PFFC's Player of the Year.

Cup competitions provided some relief from the weekly league encounters and following their promising display against Cameron Athan, there was enthusiasm for another knockout tournament. Filippo had arrived in the UK from Italy with a dream about the 'magic of the cup', and the burning ambition to play in the FA Cup. This was not easy for a Sunday League team and after exploring the complex paths that could enable PFFC to enrol in the oldest football competition of the world, he discovered that no, it was impossible for the team to do so.

Resigned to the disappointment, he always looked at PFFC's cup fixtures as an opportunity to live at least, on a smaller scale, that 'magic of the cup'. The 2002/03 season enabled him to accomplish this. In early spring PFFC were drawn to play a quarter-final in the West London Cup against Deportivo. It was not the 'SuperDepor' from La Coruña, but was still a pretty good team, way above PFFC's level.

'It's a beautiful day, don't let it get away,' the first notes of the soundtrack chosen by ITV's *The Premiership*, were echoing from the ghetto blaster of Lady Phyllis, the *maitresse* of the Regent's Park dressing rooms, when a depleted and oddly assembled PFFC squad started to gather for the match. As Filippo looked to the sky, he felt that the apocalypse must have been very close as the sun for the seventh or more day was continuing to shine and the month of March had yet to end. He wondered if this heralded the arrival of the Indian summer a few months earlier than expected. The grass on the pitch was as rare as Filippo's goals. Aware that PFFC had a weakened squad and the opponents presented a significant obstacle to the semi-finals, Ricci thought it wise to engage in some subtle psychological tricks that might undermine the opponents before kick-off. In the dressing rooms he told the opposing captain that PFFC were 'crap' and had no chance of winning. Outside, Alan Johns was putting up the nets helped by the diminutive figure of Marco 2 who, incomprehensibly, was holding the much taller Rob Adams on his shoulders. This was something that defeated the law of gravity. Could this be PFFC's day, Filippo wondered.

The Gaffer was still in Italy and many familiar faces were missing, so a last-minute recruitment plan had to be hastily organised to get the 11 or 12 men to Regent's Park. Luigi Coldagelli, Filippo's old friend, had played against PFFC in Rome in that famous match in December 2000 and, after falling artistically in the box after a generous lunge by Raj Chada, had earned the Italian national team of journalists the penalty for the final 2-2 draw. It was time for him to give something back to PFFC. In London for a fling with an ex-wife of a Wimbledon men's singles champion, he spent Saturday night in different clubs, only reaching his bed at 5am. Just three hours later his alarm went off to get him to Regent's Park on time for kick-off.

Fontana brought Stefano (another Italian who had already worn a PFFC shirt on a couple of occasions) and 'Aussie Rules John'. It was John's debut: not in PFFC's colours, but more specifically, on any football pitch. This short, stocky, blonde Australian had never played a game of football in his life. 'But I played hockey,' he said, 'so I'm fit.' That was promising, at least. 'And I also played Aussie Rules football down under, but I know that here you can't touch the ball with your hands.' Ricci was not reassured, while John was astonished to learn that opposing British football teams share the same dressing room. Filippo sympathised, but tried to explain to 'Aussie Rules John' that the atmosphere on the pitch was amicable. 'So, no red cards?' John asked, before laughing.

PFFC lined up with Ian Coyne in goal; John, Paul Kayley, Brian Bannister and Owen Mather in defence; Alan Johns, Kieran Alger, Luigi Coldagelli and Stefano in midfield; with Marco Fontana behind striker Paul Gibbins. That was the shape on paper. Aussie Rules John asked Kayley what to do with corners and Ricci what to do in general, before even trying to get his head around the offside rule. Ricci, injured since October, started on the touchline from where he tried to coach John how to take a throw-in in the European way, and not the Australian one, much to the astonishment of opponents and referee. But John was a conscientious pupil and fully committed, and on his flank that morning nothing went past him: not an opponent, a ball, or a pin. It was an Australian wall, adapted to British conditions.

Unfortunately, Marco Fontana, one of PFFC's most accomplished players, had to go off injured to be replaced by Filippo, for his first game in months. The opponents hit the bar and showed some good touches but time passed without them breaking the deadlock. PFFC's defence remained rock solid, with Alger and Coldagelli controlling midfield. Alan Johns was having one of his memorable performances on the wing before suggesting a tactical change to Filippo at half-time: why not put five in midfield to shore it up, with Gibbins as a lone striker? Stefano at this point had to return to his car to top up the parking meter with Filippo carrying on; Rob Adams went in goal, leaving Ian Coyne to reinforce the midfield.

Then the 'magic of the cup' finally happened. Coldagelli retrieved the ball in midfield and immediately sent it left to Johns, who made a powerful run and put in an excellent cross which eventually found its way to Filippo, by now gasping for air in the unfamiliar position of a number ten. The ball bounced off his tummy but fortunately straight into the path of an unmarked Gibbins in Deportivo's box. The South African controlled the ball before coolly placing it beyond their goalkeeper into the back of the net. With the little energy he had left, Filippo embarked on an ecstatic celebration before he and his team-mates rallied in a disciplined defensive line for the remainder of the game. The line was only broken with one Italian catenaccio-style counter, which ended with Coyne hitting the bar from 30 yards. Finally, the whistle went and Filippo led the celebration with a proper chant: 'One-nil, to Philosophy'.

Back in the dressing room, there was great excitement. 'We are 90 minutes away from suits,' quipped Alan Johns. Only one game separated PFFC from the final. By unanimous agreement Aussie Rules John was named man of the match; his football debut immediately became a classic in PFFC's history. 'It's a beautiful day, don't let it get away.' Once more Filippo entered Lady Phyllis's office, plugged in his hairdryer and gave a big hug to the 'Lady from Campania'. He was vindicated: yes, the cup can be magic.

With the championship won, there was even brief talk of a double. The semi-final of the cup was scheduled for 27 April on a grass pitch near Chiswick. Again, the Gaffer was away and getting the squad together presented another headache for Filippo. Coldagelli was back in Rome, but Filippo was able to introduce to the team another Italian – Gabriele Capurso ('Lele'), a young gastroenterologist who was the brother of a friend of Filippo's wife. He had just arrived in London to work and study at the Hammersmith Hospital and the following season would become a pivotal figure both on the pitch and in recruiting talented players.

The semi-final saw Raj Chada return after a nine-month absence for major surgery. PFFC were also strengthened by Puskas's availability. The main problem was the opposition. Lonsdale were far more organised than any of the teams in the Grafton League, and far superior even for a full-strength PFFC. Lonsdale duly went 4-0 up in half an hour, with Richard Shepherd pulling one goal back. Debutant Lele

Capurso came on as a substitute for Filippo but there was no magic this time: PFFC lost 6-1 and the dream of the double was gone. For Filippo, however, the 'magic of the cup' was forever cherished in his memory.

The 2002/03 season also brought the departure of Stefan Howald, who returned to Zurich halfway through. This quiet, unassuming, teetotal journalist-footballer (and future biographer and translator of Eric Ambler, Stuart Hood and George Orwell) played his first match for Philosophy Football at the age of 41. He was 50 by the time of his last outing, a vital 3-2 victory over Surbiton Strollers in which, according to script, he scored the winning goal as a second-half substitute. He was at that point PFFC's most capped and longest-serving player, the only one to have stayed the distance during its darkest times. He once refused a penalty on 'ethical' grounds, mildly correcting the referee's decision. He was rumoured to have committed a foul once, during an away match in East Molesey. Off the pitch, he had written about the team extensively in articles and newspaper columns, while his diary recorded the team's fortunes over a long period. As PFFC's original 'European' he hosted the first tour, which generated long-term friendships between PFFC players and those in his own FC Levante Wibi, for whom he continued playing once back in Zurich. He was wise counsel for the Gaffer and always held in respect by the squad, who dedicated poems and songs to him at end-of-year parties, including Filippo's adapted Italian football chant.

Segna sempre lui
Segna sempre lui
Si chiama Stefan Howald
Si chiama Stefan Howald

[It's always him to score
It's always him to score
His name is Stefan Howald
His name is Stefan Howald]

Half-Time Team Talk

Mister Gramsci, I suppose

*Egemonia, concretezza marxiana,
collettivismo sovietico.
Su questi tre pilastri l'allenatore
Geoff Andrews ha costruito
il successo di una nostra
vecchia conoscenza:
il Philosophy Football FC*

BY THE end of the 2003/04 season, PFFC could claim that it had changed beyond all recognition since its early days of heavy defeats, struggling for numbers, and gloomy pub post-mortems. The football had improved. And the philosophy meant more than words on a shirt or the odd

slogan. The club had also gained some modest public recognition, particularly in Italy where Ricci's influence had helped generate interest and curiosity. In two articles for the Italian football magazine *Linea Bianca*, an interesting, experimental project that was intended to mix *calcio e letteratura* by drawing on words from the best Italian writers and journalists (and was published in book form four times a year), Filippo first reflected on his own impressions as an Italian in London and his experience of football. Then, in an extensive, relaxed, tongue-in-cheek chat with the Gaffer, he tried to elicit from him more of his original philosophy in establishing the team and what it might now become. What role does the manager have in a philosophy football team? In the wide-ranging interview published in *Linea Bianca*, Andrews told Ricci more about how his concept of football management had an unlikely provenance in the ideas of another Italian; the Marxist thinker, Antonio Gramsci. The conversation between the two friends flowed as freely as the wine, as they revisited the ideas that for years had kept them together.

'Well, Gramsci had this concept of hegemony which I think is a good starting point for any manager. If they are to be successful, then managers have to win the consent of the players and maintain it. Hegemony was different from domination, which is based upon strength, while the latter depends upon the power of persuasion. I never liked hard, abrasive, screaming managers, ready to clash with their own players. The concept of hegemony when applied to football management means you exercise leadership in order to change the culture, the old ideas, the predefined values of a society.

'The models for English football were old, petty and outdated. Look at the job done by Arsène Wenger at Arsenal, who was then at his peak. Within a few years he has created a winning model, revolutionising the style of play at a club that had been known as 'boring boring Arsenal', a dull team used to winning 1-0. With the arrival of Wenger, Arsenal returned to winning ways but only by playing spectacular football. He started with a typically British defence (Dixon, Keown, Adams, Winterburn), but over time added a Frenchness to the team. At the same time, he asked his French players to anglicise themselves, to adapt to the indigenous football, an essential facet if you want to win in England. Putting it philosophically, his was a manifesto of concreteness as opposed to abstraction. So he followed, though without knowing it, the Gramscian model.

Gramsci argued that real political change only comes when the alternative is rooted in an understanding of the culture as well as the intellectual and social forces needed to transcend the reality. And the same with Wenger: he studied the local conditions, its reality, and made it his. It was with this insight, that he began his revolution. A masterpiece.

'Of course, Gramsci was influenced by Karl Marx who also praised "concreteness". He criticised the Hegelian dialectic because it was based on "the head", or on ideas, and not on "the feet", which represent material and economic conditions. It's a metaphor that anticipates football. Philosophical abstraction offers nothing for football. You need concreteness. You need to stick to a daily reality and study your resources and those of your opponent. For example, I like to have an Italian number ten in my team. It gives the option of playing a 4-3-1-2 system, a system that at our lowly level is enough to surprise opponents who aren't that tactically aware. At the same time, the system requires my players, with their British football heritage, to change their approach, to widen their limited tactical horizons, to adapt to a new scheme.

'And this is where hegemony comes into it. A manager must not overdo things. Abstraction plays nasty tricks. I recall a decisive game in the Grafton League against our great rivals, Inter Aztec. I decided to change the system and go for three in defence. One of the three defenders was late, stuck in traffic. This, in itself, symbolises reality, the concreteness that defies the simple thought or idea. I replaced him with another player, not suited to playing in a back three, convinced as I was of the superiority of the system, certain that it would compensate for the absence of one player. After 20 minutes we were 3-0 down. This is where what Gramsci considered the everyday experience comes into the picture: the ability to absorb the daily reality, to grasp the local culture and the social texture, so that you can make radical changes. I reverted to a back four, we won

6-4 and clinched the title. In football, too, you can't have a revolution based on abstraction.'

Ricci then asked Andrews for his views on Albert Camus, whose words were the first to adorn the team's shirts and regularly worn by PFFC's goalkeeper. How can Camus's ideas influence football?

'Camus (and Jean-Paul Sartre, another existentialist) both wanted the individual to be free to express themselves. They wanted him to enjoy more freedom, not simply to submit to the long march of history. Applied to football, this concept describes the characteristics of the postmodernist player. This is the player capable of distancing himself from the sport's deadened culture, able to exploit social fragmentation, capable of forging his own space so that he can best express himself in a free way. The postmodernist player is one who has played in different countries and teams, without particular loyalty or affection to shirts and cultures, but equally capable of adapting himself without difficulty, winning over not only his supporters but also entire countries. His identity imposes itself on concepts such as residency, nationality and loyalty. I'd put Maradona and Cantona, the last great postmodernist, in this category. At another level, I would also put Rob Adams, our long-standing goalkeeper, in this category. He plays with great freedom of expression, carrying on conversations with himself and the team, sometimes in dialogue also with the opponents, always able to adapt to changing situations and formations in front of him.'

But surely, PF had been built along strong collectivist principles?

'Collectivism is the ability to assign to individuals a precise role whereby they can best express their uniqueness, while always bearing in mind that the main aim is what benefits the group. The first two great collectivist managers in England were Bill Shankly at Liverpool and Brian Clough at Nottingham Forest. They were the first to understand the importance of protecting the group, especially its youngest members. But, of course, as Gramsci says on the shirt we wear in some of our away matches, "Football is a model of individualistic society. But it is regulated by the unwritten rule of fair play." Our players understand that very well, though perhaps in the early days they took it too literally.'

Finally, Ricci asked him whether a football team could be built on philosophy alone.

'No. Nor in life. Gramsci (and Marx) used to repeat this continuously. Philosophy must be applied to the social model and it must be rooted in the historical experience of a society. The difficulties, for a manager as for a philosopher, lie precisely in building a leadership – that is, hegemony that can adapt itself to the reality, that can win over the masses. The basic structure of a football formation is like the working class, symbolising and guaranteeing daily bread. This is the basic work rate that must be enriched by the ideas and creativity of the thinkers. A manager has to bring together these two entities, to act as intermediary, without creating hierarchies. Without the full-back, no matter how poor he is, the number ten can achieve nothing. Success comes from bringing together the players' technique, ability and physical strength with the manager's ideas and strategies. He must be capable of spotting that moment when he has to take action. The moment when theory must be applied to practice.

'Philosophy can help compensate for a physiological deficit. It's this assumption that gives birth to those great victories that small teams have enjoyed in the FA Cup, making them famous the world over. Or Greece's success at the European Championship in 2004. The Gaffer, the clever thinker, must provide his men with the intellectual means to help them overcome their technical limits. This is something that's completely different from managing an entire season, which is why upsets usually happen in the cups and far less often in the league. You have to use and exploit your own resources.

'The main difficulty for a manager is to know how to convey his thoughts to the players. There are a lot of philosophers on benches but very few are successful. The gaffer must be able to gain the consent of his players, just as an intellectual must win the trust of the proletariat to bring about a revolution. There, we're back to the concept of hegemony once more: the ability to win the hearts and minds of your own players.'

6

From Hackney Marshes to Maida Vale

THE UNLIKELY position of being two-time champions of the Grafton Millennium League stimulated further thought about PFFC's next journey. It was time for another challenge and preparations were put in place to make a historic move east to Hackney Marshes, a legendary turf graced by David Beckham among others. Before they did battle there with the bureaucracy of the Camden Sunday League (their new home), however, there was another opportunity to test their credentials as a left-wing football team. A pre-season fixture had been arranged against a team of anarchist squatters in The Hague, who had generously invited them to stay in their makeshift temporary accommodation for a game of table football prior to the match. What they didn't say was that one of their team was an international at the indoor sport and any early tactical advantage was surrendered before they had entered the dressing room.

The regular game was a different affair and the philosophers, captained by Rob Adams and with all the outfield players wearing the number 14 Johan Cruyff shirt ('Football is a game you play with your brain,' the Dutch master once said) won an exciting encounter on penalties after it finished 2-2 after 90 minutes. 'Football and philosophy united together on the turf' reported the local paper, *Haagsche Courant*. Off the pitch, the visiting philosophers were treated to a rendition of post-match poetry by the hosts and took in Amsterdam's Orange Football Museum on a sightseeing visit to the capital. In addition to temporary recruits, including Jon Iverson, a Danish lawyer from Aarhus (and scorer of the opening goal), whose style was compared to Jan Koller, the burly Czech striker, the squad included new players who had made their debut the previous season. Kieran Alger, Paul Gibbins and Bruce Oxley all worked in various parts of sports media and brought youth and energy to the team, putting in good performances with the South African Gibbins grabbing the second goal. Still finding their feet off the pitch, the younger recruits got lost along the canal only to be reacquainted when the manager, captain and senior players cruised past them aboard a pleasure steamer reverberating to the sound of jazz and champagne corks.

Back in London, plans for the new Camden Sunday League were ponderous and not helped by the retirement of key players. Notably, these included long-serving skipper Paul Kayley, whose career had metamorphosed from catastrophic depression-inducing defeats to unexpected and sweetly savoured triumphs. Having previously asked himself why he continued spending his Sundays trying to hold PFFC's sieve-like defence intact, he decided to retire 'at the top': he would be the team's most successful captain. The other major departures saw goal machine Neil James resume his amateur rugby career, while Raj Chada had embarked upon a political journey that would eventually lead him to the town hall as Camden Council's youngest ever leader. Joe Boyle had moved to Cardiff, where his partner had relocated to the university's French department. The pressures of the Sunday deadline at the *Racing Post* finally took their toll on Ian Coyne; at the same time Owen Mather was induced by his partner, an enthusiastic supporter of the Scottish National Party, to move north of the border. Apart from a solitary appearance in 2003/04, Kayley's retirement would be permanent; the last four would return in the coming years.

These exits briefly threatened the return of PFFC's oldest dilemma: namely how to get 11 fit bodies on to the pitch on a Sunday morning. The situation was complicated further by the Camden Sunday League's over-zealous officialdom which required every player to be registered, complete with identity card, several days before playing. This task was handed over to Ally Clow, PFFC's youngest player, who took on the job as secretary. Youth players in professional teams traditionally cleaned the boots of their seniors. In Sunday League they were given the task of ensuring that all players' registration forms, complete with up-to-date photos and date of birth and other personal details, are submitted, in accordance with league regulations, in the week before the match. Nevertheless, new players arrived and a much-changed team turned out. Now settled in at Hammersmith Hospital, Lele Capurso became more involved with the team. He shared Filippo's passion for the game as well as his talent-spotting skills; his recruits would be crucial for the coming campaign. Capurso would have a memorable year abroad, with football at its core, and, after borrowing the Gaffer's season ticket while the latter was in Italy, even adopted QPR as his second team (after AC Milan).

Founded in 1947, the Camden Sunday League had its home in Hackney Marshes. For Filippo, the name sounded mythical. It was the footballing equivalent of the Colosseum or the Pantheon. As an Italian living in London, it was a place you had to play at during your football career, whatever your level. Filippo first fell in love with Hackney Marshes after seeing the famous picture of those 100 (or more) pitches, all in use at the same time, all in one place, one beside the other. Regent's Park would always have a special place in his heart, but he relished the opportunity of playing a season for PFFC on the famous Marshes. He could say to Italian friends, 'I played on Hackney Marshes.'

As things turned out, it would be a briefer experience than he envisaged, and in a footballing sense both painful and frustrating. But he felt it was worth all the problems. It was like having played live at the Marquee in the late 1970s. Using the same analogy PFFC's performances would probably have resulted in them being booed off the stage. Still, they had trodden its sacred turf, like Bobby Moore, David Beckham, Ian Wright and Sol Campbell had done. Like thousands of ordinary Londoners, they slid in its mud, fell to heavy tackles, experienced millions of headers and played proper English football. In fact, PFFC didn't really know what they were doing. It was unknown territory. An inauspicious start meant Filippo had to postpone his Hackney Marshes debut because of Premier League Sunday matches. Nevertheless, after bureaucratic formalities were completed, on 7 September the team entered one of the North Side pitches for the first time to take on Archway All Stars. Despite a surprising early lead, they succumbed to a heavy defeat. It was one of the worst defeats PFFC had suffered since its earliest days. Arliss Porter, one of that summer's new recruits, overheard a downcast player of another team explain his side's loss to one of the groundsmen. 'Don't worry,' came the reply. 'It's not that bad, there was a team out there who got whipped 9-2.' It had been several years since PFFC had allowed their opponents to amass a cricket score. The following week, with Filippo and the Gaffer still missing, PFFC lost again, this time to York Way, with secretary Clow doing his best to keep the team together on and off the pitch. Despite his baptism of bureaucracy, Clow was looking on the bright side. Trailing 3-0 at half-time, he noted in his match report 'a sudden rush of excitement on the left … with a series of forays into their penalty area. Philosophy were succeeding in areas where last week they looked weak. Headers and tackles were being won all over the pitch which bred confidence throughout.' PFFC still lost 6-3.

It was another two weeks before Filippo finally got to play on Hackney Marshes. It was not the best match for a debut. An initial squad of 14 was quickly decimated with one player not registered, another failing to show and a third one arriving late. But Filippo had another problem. His wife Benedetta had to go to The Valley to cover Charlton v Liverpool (a 3-2 win for the home side with a rare hat-trick for the Jamaican Kevin Lisbie, who only scored one other goal in the entire season), so he needed to find a babysitter for their four-month old son, Gregorio. Lele Capurso, his Roman friend, was also playing so they decided that he would start the match against Boston Arms and at half-time Filippo would come on so that Capurso could take over the babysitting. This initially went to plan. Filippo emerged as a half-time substitute for Capurso, with the latter setting off for his child-minding duties. However, after less than 20 minutes, Capurso, by now heading towards Islington, received a phone call. 'It's Filippo. I'm coming home too. I've just been sent off.'

'IN THE 64th MINUTE PLAYER RICCI INTEN-TIONALLY BLOCKED A SHOT BY THE OPPOSING SIDE WITH HIS HANDS THAT OTHERWISE WOULD HAVE

GONE IN GOAL. I SHOWED MR RICCI A RED CARD AND DISMISSED HIM FOR DENYING AN OBVIOUS GOALSCORING OPPORTUNITY BY HANDLING THE BALL,' referee Mr McGarry noted in his report to the London Football Association.

A harsh and contested decision that resulted in a penalty to the opponents was made worse by a probable foul in the build-up on PFFC's goalkeeper which Filippo continued to protest fiercely. Eventually he exchanged the frustrations of football with family duties and allowed Capurso to return home.

While Filippo had at least realised his ambition of playing at Hackney Marshes, it was another organisational headache for the Gaffer who, despite being in Italy for much of the time, once again had to deal with irregular turnouts, last-minute player recruitment and waning commitment. 'Lost 3-0 on Sunday against very beatable opponents, no better than the teams we have been beating over the last two years. The defeat was ENTIRELY due to late pull-outs, non-attendance and non-registration. If we had had the squad I sent round before the match we would definitely have won this game,' he lamented after one defeat. 'Several players were available but not registered; others registered but not available,' he complained after another debacle.

In fact, non-registration was a new phenomenon and one that Ally Clow constantly had to deal with. It was a ritual that required the production of lists and ticking-off of identity cards before allowing players to take the field; this was in marked contrast to the Grafton League where even roving substitutes were permitted. The failings on

107

the pitch – five successive losses brought back memories of PFFC's earliest years – increased the burdens of officialdom.

On 19 October PFFC graced the east London grass for the last time as Filippo joined his team for the return match against Boston Arms. It ended in another 5-0 defeat and it marked the end of the club's brief encounter with Hackney Marshes. At least Filippo could take back some memories. There were the dressing rooms, designed in a similar way to those of Regent's Park: a small dressing area on the side, with the showers all lined up together in the middle of the main area. Surprisingly, he found that the taps of the showers were not placed at a normal height of two metres. Rather, they were situated at 90–100 centimetres from the ground so that to get wet players had to manoeuvre like a contortionist in order to ensure that their large frames fitted into the small space. Several times he witnessed enormous Englishmen bending in a desperate way to try and obtain some water on their heads or, failing that, at least their shoulders. Returning from the shower to the dressing room necessarily involved, as it had in Regent's Park, an obstacle course, in which the main objective was to arrive back at your clothes peg with as little mud as possible. Back then, Filippo and Capurso, the two Italians, were the only ones out of hundreds of players to wear flip-flops to achieve this objective. Even that felt like cheating. Before play had even begun, finding the correct pitch from the many was always a challenging navigational task and could take several minutes of walking and route planning. Of the five games PFFC played in the Camden Sunday League, Filippo made two appearances and took one red card. But at least he could say, 'I played on Hackney Marshes.'

Hackney Marshes was not, for Philosophy Football, a nostalgic return to one of the original environs of the people's game. At times, it seemed more like an unwelcome reminder of their fortunes in their first league season, though their new opponents had little of the charm and conviviality of the musicians. The change of league had not worked out. They had suffered heavy defeats in the past but at least teams in the Musical Association League were friendly enough; at Hackney Marshes, freed of its romantic image, you often got a good kicking in the more traditional manner. But there was a more mundane reason why a Philosophy Football team of journalists, academics, teachers, musicians, lawyers and doctors failed at Hackney Marshes. Perhaps they were just too posh.

After the difficulties of adjusting its philosophy to meet the parameters of the league bureaucracy – and, to be frank, tired of being thrashed – by October the Gaffer decided it was time PFFC abandoned the 340 acres of hallowed mud for the more salubrious surrounds of Paddington Recreation Ground in Maida Vale. 'Pad Rec' had its origins in a Victorian public park after it had been procured in the 1880s due to the efforts of its local MP, Lord Randolph Churchill, father of Sir Winston. It was the first of its kind to be used for athletics and was distinctive in its early years for its cricket pavilion and cycle tracks. By the time PFFC could call it home, it offered multi-purpose facilities with its sought-after astroturf pitches more than twice as expensive to hire as grass pitches. The venue held a particular appeal for PFFC. Some of their earliest games had been played there, when in the worst winter months Regent's Park was waterlogged. Maida Vale had also been Filippo's home when he and Benedetta first moved to London. It was there that the Gaffer had written a cheque for £1 to 'sign' Sam Dalla Bona, a regular starter in midfield for Claudio Ranieri's Chelsea who would often turn up at the Riccis' for dinner. The signing was immortalised in a picture taken at Filippo's flat in Maida Vale, and the cheque conserved as a precious memory. Dalla Bona never donned a PFFC shirt but remained part of the team's history, partly as a celebrated figure but also as virtually the only player with Chelsea connections the QPR-supporting Andrews would accommodate. The Riccis' flat had the added advantage of being within a 15-minute walk of a very good Spanish restaurant and tapas bar – Meson Bilbao – presided over by Jose, a jovial, plump and bearded Basque restaurateur.

Joining the London Midweek League, the brainchild of the amiable Hanif, an entrepreneur who seemed to make a living organising football matches, had its own challenges. The matches were played at night which brought more disappointment to some key players, including veteran goalkeeper Rob Adams who took drama evening classes, while there was little hope of Raj Chada escaping Labour Party branch meetings. Moreover, they were late entering the league and only started playing regularly from the beginning of November.

The further delay was due to the first of what would be three tours dedicated to the Italian film director Pier Paolo

Pasolini. Mick Walton, the Italian-based language teacher who had hosted the five-a-side tournament in Pordenone, had remained in touch with the team and had participated in Chada's Football in the Communities tournament in 2002. Now, he proposed another tournament to celebrate the contribution of Pasolini who in his early years had lived and worked (and played football) in Casarsa, some eight miles from Pordenone. Walton, who had made a brief appearance as an extra in Pasolini's film *The Canterbury Tales*, had been struck by a quote from the film director in a newspaper article and suggested to Hugh Tisdale the idea of a Philosophy Football shirt with its words, 'Dopo la letteratura e l'eros, il calcio è uno dei grande piaceri.' Or, 'After literature and sex, football is one of the great pleasures.' He arranged for the shirt to be presented to the mayor at the town hall, organised another five-a-side tournament and even held a brief 11-a-side practice match on the sandy pitch in Via del Fante where Pasolini himself had played more than 50 years before. Stefan Howald had brought his old FC Levante team from Zurich to participate in the tournament and so it was an international mix of Italian, Swiss and British players that celebrated Pasolini's little-known passion for football.

PFFC's late entry into the London Midweek League meant that for most of the season in order to catch up they played two matches a week – on Mondays and Wednesdays. The teams were composed of different sorts of players. Gone were the residentially concentrated teams and taking to the field instead was a mixture of companies, from the BBC to Air France and TNT Magazine, law firms and transport contractors, along with old friends South Indies who had moved there from the Grafton League.

Weekday matches meant new recruits were urgently required. PFFC also needed a new captain – journalism and politics ending the temporary armband responsibilities of Coyne and Chada – and, impressed by his administrative efficiency and growing commitment, and even more by his midfield energy, the Gaffer turned once more to Ally Clow who, at 23, was still the youngest player in the team. Clow, Lele Capurso and Filippo now put their scouting talents to good use in the drive for like-minded players. Capurso, who was based nearby at Hammersmith Hospital, brought in Eric O'Connor, an American biologist from San Diego, and Vipul Bhakta, a cancer researcher who had played in the same Leicester schoolboy team as Emile Heskey. Capurso would later add two more Romans: neurologist Giacomo Koch and lawyer Vito Vittore, part of the ever-increasing Italian émigré community from Silvio Berlusconi's country. Another recruit was Edgar Rivera, a Mexican chef and a striker with the silkiest of touches and a sharp eye for goal. Clow brought in Bryan Green, an old school-friend from Fife who had moved to London on an electrician's contract to work on the Olympic site in Stratford. He was a fast, tough-tackling and skilful player who could play either in defence or midfield. Playing twice a week after work meant the Gaffer and Filippo were on the constant look-out for new players to bolster the squad.

Therefore, the PFFC squad which took to the pitch at Maida Vale in the new league had several unfamiliar faces. Lining up in front of new goalkeeper Adrian Coates

112

was a back four of Filippo at right-back, Bruce Oxley and Bryan Green at centre-half and Vipul Bhakta at left-back. In midfield Clow was joined by Kieran Alger, Jamie Duff – an excellent all-round sportsman who had been recruited from the *New Statesman*'s cricket team, whose short stay was followed by a longer commitment by his brother Ronan – and Dan Rook, a short, skilful playmaker who chairman Tisdale likened to a young Joe Cole. The North American strike partnership of 'Eric and Edgar' was one of contrasting styles; the tireless running and wholehearted commitment of the San Diego biologist complementing the more technically gifted Mexican cook.

The early 2-2 draw with BBC Post-Production (with debut goals from O'Connor and Duff) was promising though hardly an indication of what was to come. Playing twice a week clearly added to the sense of common endeavour and was an ideal way of adhering new players to the club's philosophy, but a run of three consecutive wins was unexpected for a new team, particularly as they had been trailing in all of them. Rivera was proving a lethal finisher in front of goal, Green was dominant in midfield and Capurso a voice of authority in defence. Vice-captain Alger, another powerful presence in midfield, epitomised to the Italians all the best virtues of English football, with his non-stop work rate, strong tackles and imposing headers. His voice became such a familiar feature of the matches that Filippo wondered if the trademark shout 'Alger's up' accompanied his rise from bed in the morning or when he left his desk at work.

PFFC then produced five more straight league wins either side of Christmas, starting with a narrow 2-1 victory in which Richard Shepherd, normally a winger, played the entire match in goal without using his hands more than twice, and culminating with two more narrow victories. In three matches during this run PFFC were losing at half-time and the 'never say die' spirit was picked up by both team-mates and opponents. This run included the match of the season, a 4-3 defeat of Air France, in which PFFC had been 2-0 down at half-time. The late rally was fuelled by the return of Alan Johns, now almost of veteran status, who, typically, scored the winner. Capurso, injured but retaining his vocal presence from the touchline, hailed John's performance by comparing him to the legendary AS Roma maestro, 'As Totti! As Totti!'

In the following game, the last of the run, Capurso was once again forced to the touchlines, though this time the Roman gastroenterologist departed the scene after talking himself into two yellow cards. Resilience and consistency were crucial as in addition to being without a regular keeper Edgar Rivera had been head-hunted for a chef position outside London and Bryan Green left for New Zealand on another electrician's contract. More recruitment was needed and the production line of creative, talented and remarkably committed players kept coming. Filippo brought in Mauro Campana, a tall, pony-tailed musician, web designer and DJ from Rome (nicknamed 'Neeskens' after the former Dutch midfielder). Campana was intending to stay for only six months to learn the language but like Capecelatro and Clow he found London an ideal place to pursue his football and musical passions and, in PFFC, a convivial home outside work. Clow brought in someone he had met through work:

Damian Evans, the rock buyer at HMV in Richmond. They had played five-a-side together and Clow thought he would slot in at centre-back. In fact, Evans, who had played schoolboy football with future Welsh international Simon Davies in Pembrokeshire, was an ideal replacement for Green, with his surging forward runs and ability to sweep up at the back.

The new squad had talented players, but it was probably the camaraderie that was the crucial factor in sustaining the winning mentality. Central to this were the late post-match dinners at Meson Bilbao, which would be adopted by the team as the chosen location for parties and celebrations over the next decade. During this season it became a twice-weekly appointment for post-match fraternising and analysis, which usually went on until midnight when the last Tubes were scheduled to leave. That was well over normal closure time, but Jose, the charismatic owner, a moustached Basque from the town of Vitoria, and Josie, the patient, sympathetic and always loyal waitress, never complained that they were ready to close when a dozen football players trooped in. This was unusual for London restaurants in the inner suburbs.

On weekdays the restaurant was normally very quiet and often the team were the only customers; they would be its most regular patrons for several years. Sitting upstairs, squeezed into a corner table or around the bar, the shared dishes of chorizo busturia, patatas bravas, calamares, jamon and morcilla (a Spanish version of black pudding popular among PFFC's Lancashire contingent) became so familiar that Josie got to know each player's preferences. After a year or so Jose started semi-retirement in Spain and so for most of the nights it was Josie who looked after the restaurant. Routines were established: the meal ended with a hazelnut digestive or a more questionable Pacharan, a classic liqueur from the Basque Country, and a dessert served in a large enough portion to be passed among 12 spoons. With matches starting at 7pm, and the table taken at 9.30pm or 10pm, there were long, late digressions on the state of football, classic games from earlier years, obscure bands and music preferences. A football team was continuing to gather a disparate group of people. And it was football that kept them together. Players who left would keep in touch, returning time and again at different points for a game or to meet and talk about the club and its history. It was why the squad was able to exist for longer than the average Sunday League team.

Late-night dinners played an important part in the building of the midweek squad, for whom success had come early. They were now top and needed one final victory from their last three matches to clinch their third successive league title; a situation that was unimaginable a few months earlier in Hackney. The first of these games, against lowly Boodle Hatfield, the Mayfair law firm, suggested that nerves had taken over and they succumbed to an unexpected 3-1 defeat, the only memorable event being an unlikely headed goal from Alan Johns.

The next match, against bottom side Finchpalm, a Watford firm of railroad contractors, was anything but a comfortable climax to the season. Leading 1-0 at half-time, PFFC doubled their advantage early in the second half, only to concede with ten minutes left following a defensive mix-up. It was 2-1 and some nervous minutes followed. The team had been strengthened in recent weeks by the arrival of a 'third' Marco, a Roman who had been on Lazio's books as a junior. The Gaffer, with the unusual luxury of having four substitutes to choose from for his three changes, threw Marco on again to help see the game out. Finally, they got over the line and more celebrations ensued. The match had taken place the day before Rob Adams' 40th birthday. The veteran goalkeeper, the team's first player of the year, who had been picking the ball out of Philosophy Football's net since 1999, had returned for a final farewell performance. As the team celebrated on the pitch, however, one person was missing. The victory had come at a cost.

A wonderful night became a sad night followed by an unexpected rift which temporarily disrupted the club's celebrations and its future plans. Filippo had started on the bench and warmed up in the freezing temperature, expecting to be called on in the second half as one of the three substitutes in the crucial game. He wanted to join the party and assumed he would have an important cameo role towards the end of the game. The Gaffer, with long experience of overseeing regular defeats and the difficulty of getting 11 players on the pitch, had more recently got used to winning – inspired (ironically in this case) by Filippo's success in changing the team's mentality – and choosing from a full squad. With the unexpected recent acquisition of Marco 3, he made a fateful choice for the third and final change, leaving Filippo as an unused substitute. Filippo felt betrayed by his friend and, in typically dramatic fashion, broke from the team's jubilant celebrations at the final whistle and returned home in a rage and in some pain. He had wanted to play and felt he deserved to be on the pitch with the team at the end, not least for his enthusiasm and his overall contribution which had played a significant part in keeping the team on track as it deserted the mud of Hackney Marshes in search of glory on the well-worn astroturf of Maida Vale.

Filippo had missed the last six games of the season for work reasons. That was six games played in just three weeks of intensity and emotion. PFFC had finally become exactly what he had fought for at the very beginning of his journey with the club, three and a half years before: namely, a competitive team that had learnt to fight, to come from behind, not to surrender. A team that was by now expressing on the pitch the character that had been totally absent in September 2000. Afterwards, he reflected that the Gaffer was right. He had adopted this very Italian mentality of 'results first' that Filippo had transmitted to him during the previous successful years, and another title was at stake on that night. After all, the game was complicated: PFFC were winning 1-0 at half-time but shortly after adding the second goal they conceded and had to see out the last period of the match. In the Italian mentality, there was no room for honorary cameos but rather strong defence and discipline. The Gaffer was thinking about the game and the season. He was right.

Filippo soon regretted missing the party and rejected an initial thought of leaving the team. He had realised how much PFFC meant to his life in his adopted city. While

Filippo was coming to the conclusion that the Gaffer had been correct in his decision, the Gaffer had moved in the other direction, believing he himself had made an error which potentially jeopardised the vital spirit of the team. From different starting points they arrived at the similar conclusion that their close friendship was too important to suffer because of the incident. Moreover, the team's future prospects depended on their joint input; at times, this became a bad cop and good cop alliance; at others an organisational engine steering the club to new challenges; on other occasions reflected an almost parental concern for the welfare of their underlings.

On the Saturday night following the league victory, they were both in Camden to celebrate Rob Adams' 40th birthday. Filippo embraced the Gaffer and the following week he started the game. In goal. PFFC kept a clean sheet in a 3-0 win.

Once this brief turmoil was resolved, the squad turned up in force at the London Midweek League's end-of-season

awards ceremony at a plush west London hotel. In the end, despite their hectic fixture list and changes in personnel, they had won the league comfortably with 11 wins and 34 points from their 16 fixtures. They all received medals and the Gaffer was given the manager of the season award. It had been an eventful year and probably PFFC's most successful league campaign. In fact, they would never again reach the same heights of league success.

7

Playing Pasolini

AT THE end of what turned out to be a triumphant season after the turmoil at Hackney, attention turned once again to Europe. There were new opportunities to cement the connection with the two 'philosophers' who had meant most to the club. These were Albert Camus, whose shirt had started the whole journey, and Pier Paolo Pasolini. It was Pasolini's insight on the nature of political power in Italy that had influenced Geoff Andrews' analysis of Silvio Berlusconi. Pasolini's death under mysterious circumstances on the outskirts of Rome in 1975 gave rise to a scandal and inquisition that had still not been resolved decades later, although the occasion of its anniversary often stimulated further debate and discussion. Some claimed he had been beaten by a male prostitute; others said he was the victim of an attack by fascists or state officials in reaction to a series of critical articles he had written for Italy's main broadsheet newspaper, *Corriere della Sera*, in the months before his death. Here he demanded the ruling Christian Democrats be put on trial for corruption and collusion with the Mafia, while he pointed out that the state itself had failed to prosecute neo-fascists responsible for a series of bombings in Italian cities.

For the second time, Filippo and Luigi Coldagelli organised an impressive tour programme for Rome where they would play a match to commemorate Pasolini and to launch his PF shirt. The match was to be played at the famous Stadio dei Marmi ('Stadium of Marbles'), built in 1932 in Mussolini's time and subsequently a venue for international sporting events and prominently situated beside the Stadio Olimpico, Rome's main stadium and home to AS Roma and Lazio. The night before the match, the squad ate together at Pommidoro, the restaurant where Pasolini dined on most days, including the night he was murdered at Ostia. In the restaurant, over pappardelle al cinghiale (pasta with a wild boar sauce), they were introduced to Franco Baldini, AS Roma's technical director, who would soon take on a similar role next to Fabio Capello when the latter became England manager. A lively evening over good food and greetings with old and new Roman friends – enlivened by Alan Johns' impersonation of Frank Sinatra – ended with a presentation of the Pasolini shirt to the owner of the restaurant, where it was placed on the wall next to the framed cheque from Pasolini's last dinner, and the paintings of Italian artist Franco Pizzicannella, another regular at Pommidoro, who was eating there the evening of PFFC's visit.

The next morning was frenetic, with Filippo, now on his scooter, coordinating a series of meetings and interviews. The Gaffer read some of Pasolini's poetry for Sky Italia in front of the Roman Forum, and Filippo presented Mayor Walter Veltroni with a shirt at the Campidoglio (his office in the piazza designed by Michelangelo) watched on by Franco Sensi and Sergio Cragnotti, the presidents of AS Roma and Lazio. Finally, when all the appointments were over and the players had forfeited pizza in favour of a light lunch (with the Gaffer amazed at how far the team had come in culinary terms), the squad made their way to the venue, immediately transfixed by the beauty of the Stadio dei Marmi, with the spectacle of the Olimpico in the background.

As a child, Filippo would be taken to the Stadio dei Marmi by his mother three times a week for athletics training. Now he was excited and proud to be leading his London team back out on to the pitch in this famous stadium, with one-year-old Gregorio on his shoulder and his wife Benedetta poised at the tunnel to take the team photographs. Their opponents were a team consisting of actors who had featured in Pasolini's films, notably Ninetto Davoli, Pasolini's most loyal actor, as well as writers, journalists and former friends of the director. Philosophy

Football designer Hugh Tisdale produced two sublime sets of pink and purple Pasolini shirts for the occasion, which was kicked off by Gianni Rivera, one of Italy's greatest ever players, a winner of the European Cup in 1963 and 1969 (the year in which he won the Ballon d'Or), a member of the Italian team that lost an epic World Cup final to Brazil in 1970, and subsequently a centre-left politician. It was a treasured moment, with PFFC's players also impressed that Rivera continued to tie his laces under the soles of his boots in classic '70s style.

The team, reunited with Matteo Patrono and captained by Kieran Alger, did not repeat the performance of 2000 and were comfortably defeated. Nevertheless, it was quite a spectacle and particularly memorable for Lèle Capurso, who had returned to Rome from London at the end of the season. In London, he had played his first 11-a-side match for eight years, felt immediately drawn to the team's spirit and was now proud to be with his team-mates back in his home city. His greatest pride, however, was being introduced to Rivera, his boyhood hero, as well as playing for his English team in front of his wife and parents. The match attracted good publicity and featured in *Gazzetta dello Sport* and *Corriere della Sera*, while on the following evening (Sunday) the Gaffer and Filippo appeared on the TV programme *Goal di Notte*, on Teleroma 56, the same radical arts channel that was showing the English First Division in the 1980s, with the rest of the squad watching in the studio dressed in Philosophy Football training tops. It was a spectacularly unforgettable – and unusual – experience for a Sunday League team from London.

The match had been organised with the help of Coldagelli's boss Walter Veltroni, mayor of Rome, and, at the time, the bright hope of Italy's flailing centre-left as it struggled to deal with Silvio Berlusconi. The Gaffer was coming to the end of his book on the depressing state of Italian politics under Berlusconi but had found some respite and hope from some unexpected quarters, notably Sicily. It seemed to him – naively as it turned out – that if Pasolini was key to understanding power at the top of Italy, then Sicily offered some hope from below. He had been in Palermo to hear the earlier story of the city's revival under Mayor Leoluca Orlando's 'Palermo Spring' during the 1980s. Travelling around the island, Andrews had encountered anti-Mafia protests, as well as experiencing the breadth of this poor island's rich culture, notably its food and film history. Impressed by its energy and hospitality, he thought it an ideal place to launch another PFFC tour. With the help of his friend Natalie Guziuk and other contacts he had made along the island's eastern coast, the possibility had arisen of a fixture against a team of local musicians from Acireale, near Catania. The tour was presented in local publicity by Guziuk as 'Una partita per la pace', 'a match for peace'. Once more it involved PFFC in the politics of another country with an international focus on the contested Iraq War.

Arriving in Palermo in the early June heat, the squad, captained by Ally Clow and accompanied once more by chairman Tisdale (but containing no Italians), PFFC spent the first evening celebrating Damian Evans's birthday in a trattoria close to the Quattro Canti, one of the city's splendid baroque squares, before a tour of the Vucciria food market the following morning. Travelling in Sicily can be a challenge and, after making the mistake of taking the train rather than bus from Palermo to Catania, an additional inconvenience was incurred when the Gaffer lost all the tickets after changing trains at an obscure location.

They eventually arrived in time for dinner at a restaurant in Acitrezza, a fishing village made famous by Giovanni Verga's novel *I Malavoglia* and Luchino Visconti's neo-realist film version of it, *La Terra Trema*.

The squad had been put up at an *agriturismo* – a farm/hotel which produces its own food and wine – at the foot of Mount Etna, owned by the captain of the opposing team. The gentle pre-match banter between the squads reached a new level overnight when the Gaffer awoke to find a dagger had been inserted in his bedstead by the opposing manager. Undeterred, the squad spent a more conventional tourist morning in Taormina, the beautiful hilltop town overlooking the Ionian Sea.

After visiting the Greco-Roman theatre, they returned to Acireale to await the last member of the squad. Work had delayed the arrival of Paul Clarke, whose early morning flight to Palermo would nevertheless give him ample time to travel to Catania for the evening's kick-off. However, the main squad's earlier tricky journey across parts of Sicily's barren landscape was nothing compared to the traumas experienced by Clarkey. On taking the airport bus from Palermo he arrived in the city to find that his luggage had been stolen. Clarke remained remarkably serene when faced with the prospect of spending the weekend without a change of clothes, and appeared relatively composed even when, in the next report of his progress, he shared the news that his wallet was also missing. His journey across Sicily was subsequently accomplished without money, clothes, or a word of Italian and only completed with the help of a handwritten note scrawled by a sympathetic Italian train passenger, which explained his predicament. That he managed to do it at all was another indication of the warm Sicilian hospitality the squad experienced throughout their trip, only partially marred by the irate taxi driver who dropped him off at Acireale's Duomo, into the clutches of the Gaffer.

The squad which lined up that early evening at Stadio Giacomo Matteotti (named after the socialist member of parliament murdered by Mussolini in 1924) in Gravina, a district of Catania, had therefore been through testing pre-match preparations. It included Jez Bray from Brussels, Damian Evans on his first tour, Alger and Gibbins on their second, old hands Alan Johns and Raj Chada, with Bruce Oxley in goal. Their opponents, Stipsy King, described themselves as a squad 'under cathartic stress'; a condition that might have worsened on seeing their much younger opponents. The pitch itself was unique. It would be the first and last time PFFC played on a surface made of volcanic ash, with Etna's sporadic eruptions discharging flows of lava, with villages, towns and the city of Catania itself showered with ash.

If that was unusual, the presentation of the match officials – all dressed as priests – was also a first. However, once Ally Clow, draped in the rainbow bandiera della pace – peace banner – led his team on to the unfamiliar surface, the subsequent 90 minutes went smoothly, with Clarke defying the odds after his precarious journey by putting in a match-winning performance with two goals in a 4-2 victory. The only challenge to the moral authority of the officials was Stipsy King's tactics of adding substitutes without withdrawing players and instructing their defensive wall to bear their behinds in response to a dangerous free kick situation.

Back home in London for the start of the 2005 season, PFFC could claim it had gone some way to reconciling its philosophy with its football. More than 200 players had already worn the red (and, sometimes, white, blue or gold) kit, with the number of different PF shirts – no longer produced from Mark Perryman's kitchen table but from offices the company shared with the football magazine *When Saturday Comes* – also expanding. The team's own philosophy was more evident in the importance given to tours and the closer identification with the lives and words of the thinkers on their shirts. Above all this was the case with Albert Camus and Pier Paolo Pasolini.

On the pitch, PFFC could not repeat the successes of their championship-winning years. After taking the league title in their first season at Maida Vale, they were promoted to the Premier Division of the London Midweek League and initially struggled, leaving them near the bottom of the table for most of the 2004/05 season. The Gaffer was unimpressed and once again attributed the early setbacks to a poor approach, complaining after defeat to lowly Abbey, that it 'was an organisational shambles from start to finish'. It was a match 'we contrived to lose ... because we weren't organised and didn't play as a team ... Everybody needs to look at the table before Monday's match against Marks and Spencer. If we lose we are likely to be relegated.' However, PFFC did the double over M&S and more resilience saw them rally and pull away from the threat of relegation towards mid-table, drawing their last five fixtures and overall winning a respectable five and losing eight matches. A key part of the revival was the central defensive pairing of Damian Evans and new German signing Stefan Rulke who, aided by Filippo and Ronan Duff, provided a Welsh-German-Italian-Irish-English line.

The birthday of Philosophy Football FC was an opportunity to renew its philosophy, and to recognise that it had become more than the average Sunday League team. In early 2005, to mark the tenth anniversary of the club, a match was arranged in Wandsworth between some of the older and longer-serving players (the 'Legends') and the more recent current squad. Fittingly, both teams wore 'Camus' – Tisdale kitted the Legends in an all-black outfit with the current team in familiar red. Ten years after their first game – Andrews and Howald being the lone survivors from that day in Battersea Park – the post-match fraternising had moved on a bit, with a celebratory lunch in a nearby gastropub that was well-attended by players and friends. PFFC's food culture now triumphed over the 'crisp' mentality of earlier years. The pints were obviously still there but were now keeping company with the magnum of Italian spumante opened by Ricci and Clow at the end of the bacchanalias.

As a further homage to Albert Camus, a 'Tenth Anniversary Tour' to Paris was planned for April. Filippo organised a match against *France Football*, the long-standing weekly magazine renowned for its interviews and photojournalism and extensive coverage of European football. Its African football correspondent Frank Simon was an old friend of Filippo's and he shared the Italian's love of the continent and its football.

Travelling on Eurostar on the Friday night, PFFC arrived at the Gare du Nord with a strong and balanced squad; a mixture of the Maida Vale regulars, with the addition of Jez Bray, his Danish colleague Jon and Alessandro, the Paris-based *Gazzetta dello Sport* correspondent, whom Filippo had recruited and whose nightspot recommendations proved invaluable over the weekend. Several of the PFFC team – Ronan Duff, Vipul Bhakta, Damian Evans, Giacomo Koch and Marco Bianco – were on their first tour and they had to be inculcated into the tour mentality. Though the early night curfew imposed by the Gaffer was loosely interpreted by the British squad members, Filippo insisted that the core of the defence should room together and so Evans, Ricci and Oxley took the triple room – with Filippo protected by his left- and right-backs on either side.

The kick-off time was even earlier than the regular Sunday morning expeditions in south London and, following their early night, the squad assembled at the Parc Municipal des Sports in Issy Le Moulineaux at just after 9am local time. The sun was out and the ride along the Seine was an upgrade from the mean streets of south London. The pitch, a third-generation astroturf surface, looked inviting at first sight but proved to be wearing as the match got under way. PFFC enjoyed the best of the action but had been denied by *France Football*'s veteran goalkeeper, Bertrand. Well into his sixth decade and an engaging opponent on off the pitch, he was a true philosopher and *bon vivant*. He defied captain Alger with a remarkable save, and on his own efforts managed to keep the score at 0-0 for 80 minutes. The match was the first occasion that PFFC adopted the 'interactive match report', which had recently been introduced by *The Guardian,* among others. Goober Fox, sitting in his Shoreditch flat, was able to construct a real-time narrative of the game from texts relayed by the Gaffer on the touchline. The audience was not large, but his evocative commentary on the PFFC website meant that players and friends who couldn't make it were kept informed.

One of those keen to hear news was designer (and chairman) Hugh Tisdale, who had produced a commemorative 'Ten Year anniversary' shirt for the trip, enabling PFFC to be decked out in the France national team's colours with their opponents in all white. He also contributed a plaque for Alger to present to his rival captain, as well as a match programme. Tisdale, with his French connections, was sorry to miss the trip but, through Fox's report, was able to remain engrossed in the game, from his home at Harwich on the Essex coast.

Fox was able to relay the drama of the last five minutes to Tisdale and others. It was Marco Bianco's inspiring performance that finally took them to a 3-0 victory over the French; all the goals (two from Bianco) coming late in the game, by which time Filippo, at the heart of PFFC's defence, was badly feeling the strain. 'Philippe!' the referee called over to him. 'Oui?' 'O'n va jouer encore cinq minute.' The news that there were still five minutes left brought mixed feelings. His initial reaction – 'That's not much, *merde!*' – quickly subsided once he had evaluated the state of his calf muscles. His body was aching with cramps and the bottle with the magic salts strategically placed inside one of Owen Mather's goalposts was now of little comfort. That marauding run into the opposite box, the one and only time he had got forward, had already faded into the distant memory. From now on the best strategy was to preserve his energy and his legs.

A few minutes later and the ball was in the net. Their net. Bianco converted a great assist by Vipul Bhakta for what already looked like the winning goal. Filippo saw Bianco, the former Lazio youth product, pulling his shirt over his head like an Italian Steven Gerrard, and set off to join in the celebration, muscles tightening and his emotions running high. He no longer cared. 'Te l'avevo detto!' he shouted to Marco ('I told you so'). He knew of Bianco's real ability and was delighted that his countryman had performed on his first tour. Running to greet him now felt like a liberation. PFFC had deserved to win, after all. Marco has pulled his shirt back, meanwhile, on to his chest and was doing an 'Elvis' with the right-wing corner flag baton, which bent, cracked and finally flew away. By the time Filippo arrived shouting, 'Marcooooooo!' Bianco was hidden under a huddle of bodies having already been floored by his team-mates. The huge frame of Jon Everson, the Danish ringer, engulfed the rest and for several minutes they remained a very animated mass of bodies. Finally, releasing himself from the legs of the great Dane, Filippo launched a classic chant for Marco. Walking back to his defensive position, which seemed a mile away, he was stopped by the ref, expecting a gentle reprimand. 'The game should finish in two minutes' time. Can we add five more minutes to that?' the referee asked him in French. 'Mais oui, pas de problem,' was his magnanimous answer. He could have said no, but he knew how highly sportsmanship was valued in the British football tradition.

And the extra time brought more prizes for this sensible British compromise with two more PFFC goals, including a cross-cum-shot from Marco plus an own goal. This was very harsh on their opponents, but jubilation for PFFC, whose comfortable-looking 3-0 victory belied the close game, with the opening goal only coming in the 86th minute. Goals that had somehow got confused amid tiredness, fatigue, and the fumes of armagnac from the night before, perhaps. Or lost in translation between the negotiations with the referee and celebrations with team-mates. Courtesy of Goober Fox's interactive commentary, within minutes of the match ending the PFFC squad were reading the match report, printed out from *France Football*'s offices nearby. Frank Simon had organised a splendid event: a match on a Saturday morning, followed by a long lunch at the restaurant du stade Jean Bouin, involving both teams and a tour of the *France Football* building, the highlight of which was the photocall handling the Ballon d'Or.

But PFFC were not just there for the football. They were there for Camus, whose thoughts first prompted the idea of Philosophy Football, 'All that I know most surely about morality and obligations I owe to football.' With these words, the first PF shirt had been launched and it remained the most popular; never out of print, it continued to sell 5,000 a year and always occupied a prominent place in the company's marketing. It was also PFFC's number one goalkeeper shirt, the one worn by Geoff Andrews in the first ever PFFC match at Battersea Park in March 1995. Camus was not a great goalkeeper; his short football career, which had started at school, ended at university for the Racing Universitaire Algerois junior team when, at 18, he contracted TB. Before his death in a car crash in 1960 at the age of 47, he had shared his thoughts on football in the university's alumni magazine. While his legacy lived on in his writings, and in his famous spats with Jean-Paul Sartre, his depiction of the lonely individual was well suited to the goalkeeper (as football journalist Jim White has suggested), who often stood apart from team-mates and was subject to different pressures. PFFC's own squad historically had undergone numerous existentialist crises of its own and perhaps appropriately often lined up in the shirts of the Danish existentialist Soren Kierkegaard, as well as Sartre.

PFFC's debt to Camus (and Sartre) was clear and a return to their old haunts in Paris's Left Bank was on the tour programme. Les Deux Magots may now be more of a tourist stop but for a couple of hours some familiar names were seen in the old café, along with a bit of existentialism and some post-match commentary.

**

The year 2005 marked another anniversary which meant yet another return to Rome. It was now 30 years since Pier Paolo Pasolini had been murdered in mysterious circumstances in Ostia. More debates resurfaced on the 30th anniversary of his death at the beginning of November 2005, with Pino

Pelosi, who had originally been convicted for the killing, making new accusations that Pasolini had been beaten to death by three attackers who denounced him as a 'dirty communist'. The mayor of Rome, Walter Veltroni, called for a new inquiry. 'There was a need for the truth,' he said.

Andrews had found Pasolini's films fascinating but was also taken by the urgency and prescience of his articles in *Corriere*, and in an article 'The Life and Death of Pier Paolo Pasolini', he argued, 'His pessimistic prognosis of Italy's decay has proved to be extraordinarily prophetic.' Pasolini understood how power worked in Italy; he had virtually predicted the crisis of Christian Democracy which led to the *Tangentopoli* ('Bribesville') scandal of the early 1990s and understood the corrosion of its cultural life that would later bring Silvio Berlusconi to power. He shared this interest with Mick Walton, and after the trip to Pasolini's former home town of Casarsa the previous autumn, the team had now decided to play another match dedicated to him in Rome, the city where he made his name as a film director.

The tour was arranged to coincide with the 30th anniversary commemorations of Pasolini's death and in late October PFFC set off for their third trip to Rome. Hugh Tisdale produced another batch of Pasolini shirts and once again, the arrangements in Rome were organised by Luigi Coldagelli, head of Mayor Veltroni's press office. This time Coldagelli arranged a four-team tournament at Campo Francesca Gianni, in San Basilio, the working-class district where Pasolini had worked and set one of his films. Their opponents in this four-team tournament were the Pasoliniana, the team composed of some of his actors;

the National Team of Journalists (PFFC's first opponents back in 2000) and the team of Italian film directors, who included among their ranks Matteo Garrone, who would later make *Gomorrah* and *Dogman*, Alessandro Piva and Davide Ferraro. Among PFFC's team were some of its London Roman contingent returning to their home city.

One player named in the original PFFC squad who could not make it, however, was Luther Blissett. Filippo had got to know Blissett, the former Watford and England striker who spent a year at AC Milan in the 1980s, after they worked together as pundits on *Football Italia*. The latter was intrigued about the possibility of returning to play in Italy – if a little bemused over the circumstances – and was named in the squad, with Filippo purchasing his ticket. Unfortunately, however, he told Filippo at the last minute that he had been shortlisted for a managerial position for an obscure non-league team and remained in Britain. There was possibly another reason for his non-appearance. For a long-time the name 'Luther Blissett' has been the pseudonym adopted by Wu-Ming, a left-wing, Italian writers' collective from Bologna. It was an association Blissett himself did not welcome and playing a football match for Pier Paolo Pasolini would only have amplified this connection. In the future, PFFC would turn out monthly in the Three-Sided Luther Blissett League in Deptford, south London.

Despite Blissett's non-appearance, the 'partita per Pier Paolo' gained great coverage in Rome. News of the match, before and after the event, reached many Italian newspapers and the Gaffer was intrigued – and not a little surprised – to

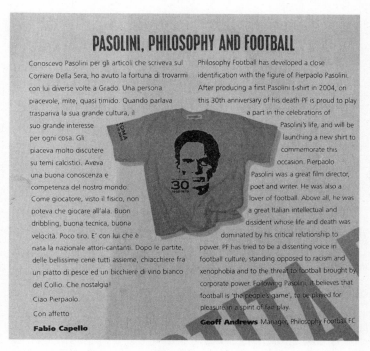

PASOLINI, PHILOSOPHY AND FOOTBALL

Conoscevo Pasolini per gli articoli che scriveva sul Corriere Della Sera, ho avuto la fortuna di trovarmi con lui diverse volte a Grado. Una persona piacevole, mite, quasi timido. Quando parlava traspariva la sua grande cultura, il suo grande interesse per ogni cosa. Gli piaceva molto discutere su temi calcistici. Aveva una buona conoscenza e competenza del nostro mondo. Come giocatore, visto il fisico, non poteva che giocare all'ala. Buon dribbling, buona tecnica, buona velocità. Poco tiro. E' con lui che è nata la nazionale attori-cantanti. Dopo le partite, delle bellissime cene tutti assieme, chiacchiere fra un piatto di pesce ed un bicchiere di vino bianco del Collio. Che nostalgia!

Ciao Pierpaolo.

Con affetto

Fabio Capello

Philosophy Football has developed a close identification with the figure of Pierpaolo Pasolini. After producing a first Pasolini t-shirt in 2004, on this 30th anniversary of his death PF is proud to play a part in the celebrations of Pasolini's life, and will be launching a new shirt to commemorate this occasion. Pierpaolo Pasolini was a great film director, poet and writer. He was also a lover of football. Above all, he was a great Italian intellectual and dissident whose life and death was dominated by his critical relationship to power. PF has tried to be a dissenting voice in football culture, standing opposed to racism and xenophobia and to the threat to football brought by corporate power. Following Pasolini, it believes that football is 'the people's game', to be played for pleasure in a spirit of fair play.

Geoff Andrews Manager, Philosophy Football FC

discover that the team he had hastily assembled for a kick-about in Battersea Park ten years earlier was now referred to by one paper as 'the famous squad of British philosophers'.

On the pitch PFFC initially lived up to expectations, trouncing the Italian film directors 4-0, with a brace from Clarke (impressing once again in Italy) and other goals from Alger and Campana (on his return to Rome). Clarkey's performances attracted the attention of some journalists, one of whom compared him to Tony Morley, Aston Villa's former tricky winger. The final against the Pasoliniana was at a crucial stage when Clarkey, in on goal, was fouled, stumbled, and in trying to retain his balance, skewed the chance. With PFFC well attuned by now to Italian ways on the pitch, the post-mortem following their eventual defeat on penalties centred on the moral and philosophical dilemma that was laid literally at Clarkey's feet: to go down and take the penalty or to show some British stiff upper lip and carry on valiantly.

The 2005/06 league season was a struggle that turned into a relegation battle. Despite an impressive victory in the first match against eventual Premier Division runners-up Alba, there were some heavy defeats, including two by 6-1, a 7-0, and even a 9-4 hammering by Warner Brothers. Nevertheless, some vital points at the end of the season were sufficient to avoid the drop, even if a goal difference of -47 brought back some troubling reminders of the early days. More recruits brought another group of Italians from the Sondrio area of Lombardy into the squad, including Marco Casparri, the 'fourth' philosopher named Marco (and a fine cook and gardener), who would be the regular stopper for the next two seasons. However, the season was more marked by the shocking news that Filippo would be leaving London to go to Madrid to be *Gazzetta dello Sport*'s correspondent in Spain. It was the end of an era for him and at the time seemed like it could be the team's finale. His farewell note was a mixture of sadness, nostalgia and irony.

Ode to Grass

Saturday afternoon, usual fucking drizzle at Stamford
  Bridge
Rain graciously hammering the grass like the Blues with
  Pompey
A message from Damian, a Welshman worried by the
  weather
In the press stand you think of mud, of tackles, of wet
  jumpers for goalposts
Of English football, as we see it from the continent
Incredibly far from Roman's millions
You fall asleep dreaming of Regent's Park. Shanks for the
  memories

Morning. The light from your bed, a sign
The sun, the clear air, the memories of the mountains in
  Italy, years rolling back
And rolling even further with Big Jack on the back of the
  moped
He's wearing shorts, not even a Geordie would dare
Bloody freezing, an unhinged two wheels, many fucking
  miles to cover
Notting Hill, Maida Vale, Lord's, Regent's Park. No traffic,
  it's Sunday morning
Gaffer coordinating the reunion. Everybody lost, scattered
  everywhere
Then you see him, his gestures, unmistakable. One in a
  million
Back to where he belongs, even without his bike
Where we belong

No nets to put up, changing rooms under the ground, no
  Lady Phyllis

But the atmosphere, the odours, the air, the 'Dolomites'
    inside the zoo
And the grass. Uneven, muddy, threadbare, faded
Alive and kicking, not dead like the astroshit
You run, up and down. Feeling your legs weighed down by
    the same grass
You dribble, one, two, three. And then you lose the ball
You shoot, unluckily very wide
You do the sombrero
You don't score, but this has nothing to do with the grass
That gives you wings, and a smile
That makes you dare, and happy
You may even think that London is a wonderful place. Innit?

8

Slow Foot

FILIPPO'S DEPARTURE to Spain was a blow. The partnership between him and the manager had been the catalyst for PFFC's revival. However, as it transpired, Filippo's move to Madrid prompted the pursuit of new directions for the club with more European tours and participation in political causes. The stronger identity forged through friendship also helped bring it closer to the original aim of being a bit more than a football team. In the last years of PFFC, this identity was strengthened further through Filippo's Spanish connections, more cultural interventions (including the unlikely overlaps between football and food) and above all – at the time of tumultuous change in the football world – by a philosophical interrogation of the game.

Unsurprisingly, soon after his arrival in the Spanish capital, Filippo organised a tour of Madrid – the club's first of many visits to Spain and its 13th European trip – in November 2006. The squad that assembled was its strongest to date, with the two full teams enough to fill a coach. The tour marked the 70th anniversary of the outbreak of the Spanish Civil War, when a mixture of generals in the military, together with religious conservatives, monarchists and fascists in the Falange (FET y de las JONS) party, declared war on the democratically elected left government of liberals and republicans and their socialist and communist allies. The previous spring PFFC had hosted a 'Never Forget, Never Again' anti-fascism tournament in London, involving (among others) Sant'Onofrio, a like-minded left-wing team from Rome which featured some of PFFC's occasional players including Matteo Patrono and Marco Capecelatro (now back in Italy). The tournament, won by PFFC's younger squad, was followed by a raucous post-match meal at Meson Bilbao – the entire ground floor area taken up with three football teams and partners, and enlivened by speeches and renditions of 'Bella Ciao' and other partisan songs. The anti-fascist Popular Front was evident in Tisdale's series of Philosophy Football designs, produced in commemoration of the Spanish Civil War and to mark the contribution of the International Brigades who had travelled to fight in defence of the republican government.

Filippo had adapted quickly to life in Madrid and joined an impressive milieu of foreign journalists and correspondents. After his experience with PFFC in London, he was anxious to continue playing regularly and sought another suitable team in the city. In fact, it became clear that he would have to build his own team, trying as much as possible to import the PFFC ethos to his new team-mates. He knew from the Gaffer's experience that any initial enthusiasm could be thwarted by serious organisational difficulties. He wasn't sure what to expect in Madrid and whether he could adapt his philosophy. And he did not have the advantage of the kind of tip offered to him in Accra, Ghana, by Ian Coyne way back in 2000.

However, he did work with football journalists, and as soon as he arrived, he began to construct a team from the press stands of the Bernabéu and the Vicente Calderón. Having spent the previous six years in London and because of the lack of Italian journalists in Madrid, he was inevitably drawn towards the English contingent, which had been strengthened by the presence of a certain David Beckham who had been at Real Madrid since 2003. Sid Lowe, the *Guardian* correspondent, was the perfect match for the much-missed figure of Andrews. Nevertheless, a team with a strong international contingent soon entered a seven-a-side tournament organised by the Madrid council. It consisted of a Danish goalkeeper, two Englishmen, and a core of talented Spanish journalists. Two characters stood out: Rene Ramos, the elder brother of Real Madrid's captain Sergio, a former player who after failing to make it as a professional footballer decided instead to become the agent of his talented brother; and Claire Rourke, a Liverpool journalist (and fan) who worked for the English channel on Real Madrid TV. Claire had played for the Doncaster Belles youth team in England. Later she returned home to become a renowned face on the Liverpool TV channel.

Fielding a talented and good-looking girl in a male-only team in quite a rough tournament was Filippo's homage to the PFFC spirit, something that would distinguish the team he had promptly named 'Philosophy Football Madrid'. Once more he had help from chairman Hugh Tisdale who designed a special version of the famous Camus shirt, with the quote now translated into Spanish. The players wore a classic red kit, and an away strip of immaculate white. As might be expected both were uniquely adapted to the Madrid conditions. PF Madrid did impressively well in their first season only to lose the tournament on disciplinary grounds. Arriving at the penultimate match against the leaders second in the table, they thought they had won the league with a convincing 4-1 victory, until three minutes before the end of the game Rene Ramos got himself involved in a pointless and inopportune tussle with the opponents, who had provoked him hoping for the kind of retaliation that he duly provided. Compared to six years of flying tackles in the London Sunday Leagues this did not strike Filippo as serious or at all surprising. 'Handbags' would have been the word used by an English newspaper to describe the incident. The game ended, and PF Madrid celebrated wildly. There was one game to go and now the trophy seemed a formality.

On the following Wednesday the disciplinary panel published its verdict, and punished Rene with a two-year ban. Filippo, as manager, made frantic phone calls; he wrote, appealed, shouted, and even threatened journalistic action. All to no avail. The verdict wasn't changed. Still in defiance of the draconian measure, Filippo then selected Rene for the last game. True, he was a 'bit of a nutter', in the English parlance Filippo had learnt in London, but as part of the PF Madrid team, he felt he deserved their full solidarity against an unfair decision. Once the opponents on the day made it clear to their rivals for the title that Rene was playing, they fielded a case for ineligibility and despite having won easily on the pitch, PF Madrid were punished with a 3-0 defeat by the disciplinary panel. That cost them the title and Filippo promptly withdrew PF Madrid from the league.

However, Filippo was determined to keep on playing and one year later established a new team from an even wider cohort of foreign journalists, including players from England, Scotland, France, Denmark, Italy, Argentina, the Basque Country and Madrid. He entered them for the Liga de Medios, a tournament dedicated to the various journalist teams (where they would remain for four years). They were quickly dubbed the X-Men because their identity cards all began with that letter. They were still using the PF Madrid Camus shirts, and in the first year reached the semi-finals of what was a highly competitive tournament thanks to an extraordinary campaign sustained by a remarkably good French goalkeeper and the prolific finishing of the Reuters correspondent, Iain Rogers, who hailed from the Isle of Man. Rogers was known to the other players as the 'Silent Killer' because he never spoke, either on or off the pitch. Never. Sid Lowe was still there, now a constant presence and sounding board for Filippo when tactics and personnel needed to be discussed. To the X-Men, Filippo re-introduced the old PFFC habit of the rotating match report written by one of the team and compiled at the end of the season in the 'review'; PFFC had published annual reviews since 2002.

The X-Men were a unique team in Madrid and continued to win against the odds, reaching the semi-finals of the tournament in a season which owed more to heart, character and philosophy than pure footballing ability. They were much weaker technically than the other teams, though were helped by a cameo appearance by the former Argentinian international Santiago Solari, who used to play for Real Madrid and Inter Milan and went on to be Real's manager. Solari helped them to a 6-1 victory, with the handsome and skilful Argentine scoring five goals. It was his one and only appearance for the X-Men and he never made himself available for selection again.

Thus, it was the X-Men and like-minded teams who provided the opposition in PFFC's latest tour, with Filippo happy and nostalgic to be reunited with his former London team-mates. It was to be a three-team tournament, to be held at Ciudad Deportiva, home of the training venues of Real Madrid's Galacticos, not far from the Bernabéu on the outskirts of the city, and guarded by a protective fence. It was an impressive complex, with the extensive range of facilities reminding some of the philosophers of their earlier match at La Borghesiana in Rome; on the other hand, its dressing room, medical centre and canteen vastly exceeded Lady Phyllis's Regent's Park changing rooms. Among the journalists' team were a Danish goalkeeper, Rene Ramos, and two British journalists, including, of course, Sid Lowe, who was by now a close friend and colleague of Filippo. Lowe was also ideally placed to participate in a tournament commemorating the outbreak of the Spanish Civil War given he had originally arrived in Spain as a PhD student, undertaking research for his thesis on the origins of Francoism. His PhD was subsequently published as a book, *Catholicism, War and the Foundation of Francoism*, though many years after he had arrived in Spain and by which time he had become a full-time football correspondent. He was a natural and like-minded ally of Filippo and shared PFFC's philosophy, while keen to revive his own football career.

On the pitch, PFFC's Legends could not quite match the performance of the London tournament, but put up some spirited resistance through a mixture of Coldagelli's elegance (he had travelled from Rome) on the ball and Big Brian Bannister's muscular defending, which brought him into several clashes with Ramos in the game with the journalists. Despite pre-tournament warnings that Spanish referees would curtail any aggressive tackles, the matches produced feisty encounters, belligerent defending, and individual skills. Bannister's bruises confirmed to many of his team-mates that you can take the player out of Regent's

Park but not Regent's Park out of the player. The Legends were no match for PFFC's current team who also defeated the journalists (despite further robust tackling from Ramos) to be the overall winners.

As with previous trips the tournament was the centrepiece of a weekend rich in culture and food, notably the chance to see Picasso's *Guernica* up close in its own room in the Reina Sofia Museum. His capture of the horror of the atrocity committed in that town made clear Italian fascist and German Nazi support for Franco and remained as evocative as it was to the 1930s generation of anti-fascists. Football remained at the heart of things, however, and Sunday evening was spent watching David Beckham play for Real Madrid against Celta Vigo. Tickets for the game had come courtesy of Franco Baldini and were delivered to the team by Chendo, the long-standing Real Madrid and former Spanish international right-back who was now a delegate at Real. Later, to complete another unusual day in the life of a Sunday League team, they enjoyed a late supper in Fabio Capello's favourite restaurant, Meson Txistu.

Here, they found Real Madrid manager Capello in one secluded corner while Fabio Cannavaro, who like his boss had recently joined Real Madrid after abandoning Juventus in the aftermath of the *Calciopoli* scandal that led the 'Old Lady' to be relegated to Serie B, was seated with his family in another spot. Damian Evans, PFFC's centre-back, was briefly introduced to Italy's World Cup-winning captain and future Ballon d'Or winner – a notable highlight for the Welsh defender, who is a great admirer of Italian football. By now well-accustomed to Spanish food from their regular gatherings at Meson Bilbao, they took their chance to eat well, late into the night at Madrid's restaurants and bars. The biggest challenge was prompted by the belated discovery that Big Brian Bannister thrived on a vegetarian diet and he needed all Filippo's tactical nous to negotiate his way through the menus of a meat-driven city. For the rest of the squad, it was *jamon* today and tomorrow.

Getting two full squads to the Spanish capital was one thing; getting 14 players out on wet weekday evenings to west London proved to be more challenging. Despite the arrival of more Italians from the alpine town of Sondrio – Andrea del Marco and Rinaldo Puccia – there was a lack of consistency throughout the league campaign. The team was further weakened by the return to Rome of Giacomo Koch – a powerful midfield presence – midway through the season. In all 33 players were used and left-back Owen Mather often had to deputise between the sticks when veteran keeper Rob Adams was busy teaching his drama and acting classes. Paul Clarke, with 15 goals, was the stand-out player, while the contrasting styles of Damian Evans, the fast, skilful, ball-playing centre-back and the imposing figure of Brian Bannister orchestrated a much-improved defence.

Once more they found the prospect of a European trip more alluring, and a younger squad set off for Lisbon over the Easter holidays. Carlos Morais, a Portuguese EU colleague of Jez Bray, was able to guide the squad around the bars and restaurants of the Bairro Alto. These late evenings proved to be a respite from the match itself where, despite being smartly turned out in the Eusébio shirt – 'Black or white we have football under our skin' –

PFFC succumbed to a 5-1 defeat against slick opponents. Remarkably, however, and in the spirit of some previous tours, the key action was off the pitch. Having adopted a good local bar near the hotel following rumours that it was one of Eusébio's favourite haunts, they were astonished to find the great man himself – the 'Black Pearl', Benfica's greatest player and one of the world's greatest strikers (733 goals in 745 competitive matches) – propped against the bar. Kieran Alger, quicker off the mark on this occasion than he had been on the pitch, was able to present him with his own Philosophy Football shirt. In a few months PFFC players had the opportunity to take pictures with the Ballon d'Or at *France Football*'s headquarters, and to meet the previous winner of the golden trophy, Cannavaro and Eusébio.

It was a poignant ending to a trip that was more memorable for the food than the football. Under Carlos's direction, players had become acquainted with yet more unfamiliar species of seafood and, following Madrid and post-match dinners at Meson Bilbao, had settled easily into various tapas combinations. Over the years, things had moved on somewhat from the inauspicious packet of crisps and a pint. Food had become an inseparable part of the PFFC experience, one that was augmented and refreshed by Italian, Spanish and other cuisines. Food (and drink) kept the team together, increased the camaraderie and opened new cultural horizons. The food and football connection reached another level, however, with their next trip to Italy.

Oltre ai formaggi, i greci servono gran gol

Slow Foot

Un altro calcio è possibile? Il gioco «lento» è un ricordo del passato

While Ricci was relocating from London to Madrid, Andrews was relocating from his Italian base in Bologna to Bra, a small town in Piedmont, some 30 miles from Turin. He had finished *Not a Normal Country*, his book on Silvio Berlusconi's impact on Italy. In later years Berlusconi's populism was mirrored in different ways by the likes of Donald Trump and Nigel Farage, but at the time the Milanese entrepreneur-turned-politician was a one-off. As owner of large sections of Italy's media as well as AC Milan, he claimed he had been obliged to 'take the field' to address the failures of Italy's political class, and thereafter presided over a serious degeneration of Italy's politics and culture. Andrews had covered Italy's demise under Berlusconi but along the way had also found some hidden voices, which suggested an alternative Italy. He now turned his attention to one of these. The Slow Food movement, whose banner he had seen for the first time in Genoa during the tumultuous G8 protests in 2001, had been founded by Carlo Petrini in the late 1980s, when he and a group of like-minded friends held a protest, armed with bowls of penne, outside a McDonald's near the Spanish Steps in Rome. Petrini was from Bra, a provincial town of 25,000 people not far from the Langhe hills, which produced some of Italy's best red wines. Petrini, an anarchic, charismatic ex-communist, who had previously set up a pirate radio station, organised a music festival and been elected as a local councillor, now installed Slow Food's HQ in the same town. By the time Andrews moved there it had grown to be the second-largest employer in town, with over 100 people on the books. It had also established the University of Gastronomic Sciences in nearby Pollenzo, while its series of international meetings of food producers at Terra Madre and the Salone del Gusto, held in the Fiat building in Lingotto, were enormous events and influential on food policy-makers.

Slow Food stood for what it called 'good, clean and fair' food, while promising to celebrate the 'simple pleasures' of convivial eating. Typically, its meetings combined a splendid dinner of local produce with a serious talk about the need for sustainable farming. One of the regular events it organised was the biennial festival – simply called Cheese – held in Bra itself, which brought together cheese producers from all over the world while convening workshop discussions on the future of sheep farmers and the virtues of raw milk. For five days the small town was taken over by cheese stalls, tastings and dinners. There was a lot of socialising and evenings could be spent with its very own 'Blues' night; listening to jazz while sampling Stilton, Roquefort and Gorgonzola.

By the time of its 2007 festival, Andrews had taken an apartment in the town and was meeting regularly with Slow Food organisers and editors. Among these was John Irving, a Carlisle-born writer, editor and translator at SF's publishing house, whose expertise on the history of Italian football surpassed even his knowledge of Italian food. At these regular lunches at Badellino's, a local hotel and restaurant in the town, the idea was conceived of holding a 'Slow Foot' tournament during the Cheese festival. The term 'Slow Foot' had recently been taken up by Italian journalists who, perhaps inspired by the Slow Food movement, sought to apply the same principles of sustainable and anti-corporate approaches to the world of football. At Badellino's, football and food were the two main topics of conversation for Andrews, Irving, Giovanni Ruffa and other locals, and there seemed a natural fit between PF's philosophy and the idea of 'Slow Foot'. After all, PFFC, in theory at least, attempted to uphold the ideals of 'good, clean and fair' football and to celebrate the game's own 'simple pleasures'. In Badellino's the proposal was made for a four-team tournament of like-minded squads.

Moreover, 'Slow Foot' was not just a humorous play on the words of the international food movement but an interesting and intriguing concept itself. It became the title of a regular column written by John Irving and Giovanni Ruffa for Matteo Patrono's sports pages in the left-wing newspaper *Il Manifesto*. The concept, which sought to put the brakes on the rapid commodification of football by arguing for a stronger fan focus and greater appreciation of the authentic historical traditions of the game, was subsequently taken up by the columnist Gianni Mura, a key figure in the Italian discussions of football, cycling, food and wine, in *La Repubblica*. Andrea De Benedetti, another occasional *Il Manifesto* writer, established a Slow Foot cultural association. John Irving later explored his love for the traditions of the beautiful game in his book *Pane e football* (Bread and Football) which drew on his experience as a young Carlisle United supporter in the 1960s and 1970s, before moving to Turin in 1977 in the midst of student protest and 'the years of lead'.

More challenging than the draw, carried out over *grappa* under the watchful eye of owner Giacomo Badellino, were the arrangements in putting together the tournament. How to find teams with food connections? Fetamania, a squad of ex-professional Greek footballers who now worked together as part of a feta cheese co-ooperative, were ideal opponents, and Stefan Howald's FC Levante Wibi, originally founded from a 1970s co-operative restaurant, were also up for it. The final team took a little longer, but after more negotiations involving Luigi Coldagelli and Matteo Patrono, the Italian Writers FC, Osvaldo Soriano (one of PFFC's opponents in San Basilio) emerged to fill the slot. Osvaldo Soriano was named after the exiled Argentinian writer and critic; a lover of football and film and promoter of democratic left-wing causes and was managed by 60-year-old Paolo Sollier, the celebrated Trotskyist intellectual who turned out for Perugia in Serie A in the 1970s. The philosophy and politics of 'Slow Foot' appealed to this squad of left-wing Italian writers. With the line-ups complete, the draw was made in Badellino's for the first (and probably last) Slow Foot *torneo*.

The tournament was listed next to tasting events and chef demonstrations in Slow Food's official 2007 Cheese programme, and after the stadium and referee were all booked, the squad arrived in the hills of the Langhe region. Renowned for its Barolo wine and numerous mountain cheeses, the pre-match meal was a rather heavy affair: a five-course *degustazione* ('tasting') at Le Torri. One of Carlo Petrini's many founding Slow Food principles was that the best wines should be available to everyone and Barolo was certainly democratised that evening in the village of Castiglione Falletto.

The *torneo* was preceded by a round-table discussion in the courtyard outside John Irving's office (his desk surrounded by shelves of wine instead of books) involving football writers and players, including John Foot, as well as Patrono, Ricci, Howald, Andrews and Pantelis Rapankis from Fetamania. John Foot, the author of *Calcio: A History of Italian Football*, and an on-loan striker for the philosophers in the *torneo*, described the 'crisis' engulfing the world of football; with big money effectively deciding the destiny of winning teams, the growing imbalance between clubs and the dull predictability of the top leagues. In the process, traditional football as a working-class sport had been distorted and replaced by a mundane language and culture which was turning top-level professional football into a soap opera. Howald, after comparing the Swiss liking for cheese with holes (Gruyère) to the frequent gaps in his national team's defence, went on to explain that his club's name was derived from the combination of a restaurant (Levante) where some players worked during an annual summer festival and the abbreviation of an address, Weinbergstrasse (Vineyard's Street), where others lived and drank wine together. Here in Bra, in a break from the musical offerings of Giuliana Palma and the Bluebreakers, local bands and orchestras and preceding a Radio Flash DJ slot, the concept of 'Slow

Foot' was theorised, scrutinised and debated, with the hope that the afternoon's tournament would produce 'good, clean and fair' football on the pitch.

The PFFC squad featured some familiar faces plus a tour debut for Rob Cawston, a digital editor recruited by Clow from the online political website Open Democracy. Once again, they lacked a regular goalkeeper so Valentina, of the Torino women's side – and a friend of Matteo Patrono – was called in at the last minute. The tournament took place at the main stadium Attilio Bravi in Viale Madonna dei Fiori, a short distance from the centre of Bra. Poignantly, it started in a very pedestrian manner, with the aged officials taking a long time to appear after lunch before finally arriving over the horizon immaculately turned out in matching kit. The first semi-final saw the Italian writers, led by Paolo Sollier (whose clenched fist salute was an iconic image for left-wing footballers in the 1970s and featured on the cover of his autobiography *Calci e sputi e colpi di testa* ('Kicks and spits and headers'), line up against the Greek feta cheese producers. This match was very one-sided, with Pantelis impressing down the right flank for the Greeks and some flowing moves from the writers, but the Osvaldo Soriano defence reflected the nature of the Swiss cheese alluded to by Stefan a couple of hours earlier and the match ended in a convincing 4-0 victory for the Greeks. The second semi-final brought PFFC up against their old and friendly Swiss opponents and the match was a tight and tense affair, which the Londoners won by the only goal. There was no leaky Swiss defence which on this occasion resembled a strong Cheddar rather than a mild Emmental.

The Swiss, however, won the third-place play-off easily, coasting to a 3-0 victory. There was growing interest and expectation for the final between PFFC and Fetamania. The Greek ex-professionals were the favourites but PFFC put up some spirited resistance in the first half with Luigi Coldagelli and Bryan Green (reappearing after years working abroad) outstanding, and Alan Johns causing problems cutting in from the left. Half-time came with the philosophers trailing by the only goal but the temperature of the match was increased right at the beginning of the second half when the Greeks tested goalkeeper Valentina direct from the kick-off with a superlative long-range strike. This put them 2-0 up but prompted an angry response from PFFC players who questioned the 'unfair' tactics of their opponents which they felt were against the spirit of the game. It destroyed PFFC's concentration and produced a bad-tempered finale. It also gave added significance to John's Foot's warnings about the impact of professionalisation on the beautiful game. The game had been won by a good, clean strike. Whether it was fair was highly debatable. Fetamania, after claiming their victory, then departed for Greek night at Cheese. 'Slow Foot' discussions continued late into the night at Badellino's, with much attention given to *Calciopoli*, the ongoing Italian football corruption scandal.

With PFFC's political philosophy and commitments more evident than in the past, there was a further opportunity to link football and protest at the end of another season of mixed league success in Maida Vale. The May events of 1968 had some resonance for a football club that had tried to be counter-cultural and, in Stefan Howald, a former player who had strong connections to the movements which had grown in the 1970s. At the end of May 2008 – the 40th anniversary of *Les evenements* – Howald organised the second PFFC trip to Zurich. On its first European tour back in June 2000, the team had been comprehensively defeated by FC Levante Wibi, with PFFC's shortcomings on the pitch reflecting its mediocre league performances. Nobody then cared much about the score, while in those innocent days of moderate centre-left governments there was a gentle optimism that Europe would be an all-embracing political entity capable of providing prosperity and stability.

By 2008, things had changed dramatically. The global financial crisis of that year was already having an impact with austerity policies, clashes over immigration and new waves of protests. Populists of left and right won unlikely victories at the polls. The new tournament in Zurich was thus appropriately (and optimistically) announced as the 'Where the Spirit Blows' competition. The choice of rival teams signified the counter culture. FC Levante Wibi belonged to the Progressive Swiss Football Association, which had been set up in 1977 following a match between a team of anarchists and a squad composed of players who had previously attempted to infiltrate the Swiss army. Their opponents in the Progressive Swiss Football Association were drawn from left-wing parties and social movements and were of mixed gender (a tradition FC Levante Wibi had maintained), played without studs or referees, with the rules negotiated and argued about and finally resolved between players in open discussion on the pitch. It was not unusual to find teams playing barefooted and even though some of the experiments were later abandoned in the cause of winning matches, many of the original players remained in 2008.

Also in Zurich were Balon Mundial, a squad founded from a team of refugees and immigrants in Turin, some of whom had escaped to Italy from strife in their own countries. Their participation through football reflected the importance of distinctive cultural identities in a global Europe, while enabling to make effective challenges to racism and discrimination. It became part of the Common Goal organisation sponsored by Spanish footballer Juan Mata and which subsequently accommodated community-based football teams around the world. For this occasion, PFFC played in a 1968 shirt designed by Tisdale which commemorated the situationists, one of the key movements in the 1968 protests. The shirt was inscribed, under an image of a clenched fist, with one of the memorable slogans of that time, 'Be Realistic, Demand the Impossible'. As far as PFFC was concerned, the politics of protest and the influence of anarchism was evident in their performance on the pitch, as much as the activities off it. Perhaps in another context, they were reunited with some of the symbols of '68. Some ill-disciplined play, frustrated gestures and occasional expressions of individualism combined to bring successive defeats and a wooden spoon.

Much had happened to the club since their last visit to Zurich eight years before – Alan Johns was the only surviving player from that trip – with three league titles and a greatly improved quality in the squad. Yet any spectators who were present at both events would not have seen much evidence

of a transformation in the team's performance. The combination of beautiful surroundings, a younger and, on paper more talented group (which was enhanced by the tour debut of Filippo's five-year-old son Gregorio), should have produced a better outcome. But the team did not impress.

The tournament, which brought together football and politics, ended with an evening cabaret event – Europe Calling: Football and the culture of protest – held at the nearby Sogar-Theater. Political commitment remained important for many in the squad. Having joined the club while doing his teacher training, left-back and most-capped player Owen Mather now taught government and politics, while active in his union and in local campaigns. He saw playing for PFFC as a continuation of his political ideals. For him, 'Ideas and action were at the heart of what PFFC do on or off the pitch and that is what I took most from being a member of this football club more so in fact than any other "regular" team that I've ever played for.' This was the case, 'Whether we were winning a league title, travelling to northern Italy to support a local mayoral candidate in a football tournament or collaborating with Whitechapel Art Gallery to conceive three-sided football at the 2010 UK general election.'

Raj Chada, a ball-winning, battling midfielder, was the most politically active of all PFFC's players, rising from councillor in 2002 to becoming leader of Camden Council at 32 in 2005. After losing his seat in 2006 he returned to his job as a leading defence lawyer with Hodge Jones & Allen, representing some of the left's most high-profile movements, including Occupy, UK Uncut and Extinction Rebellion.

Joe Boyle, right-back and PFFC's main match reporter, combined being a house dad with freelance writing, charity and local activism, getting himself elected to Cardiff City Council where he became leader of the Liberal Democrat group.

Midfielder Jez Bray only played one full season, 2000/01, for PFFC before moving to work for the European Commission in Brussels. When he was not touring with PFFC he played football for one or other of the Commission's teams, at one time winning the interdepartmental Schuman Trophy on penalties. He also found himself standing in local elections on the Change Brussels civic list, a loose centre-left grouping which also included Flemish socialists. It wasn't PFFC's politics that sustained him but its role in instilling an international outlook on life which gave him the 'confidence to feel more comfortable about living outside the UK'.

Individual political loyalties aside, PFFC's own philosophy had mellowed and, like the squad on the pitch, was in need of renewal. Not for the first time Filippo and the Gaffer wondered if the marriage between 'philosophy' and 'football' was coming to an end.

9

Three-Sided Football

THE DISAPPOINTMENT of the footballing aspects of the
Zurich tour suggested that an era might be coming to an
end. Over the years the football had improved, international
tournaments had broadened horizons and PFFC had

finally reconciled philosophy with football. Well, to some degree anyway. Was there anything else to do? Some of the regulars had taken on more family and other commitments and Sunday matches had suddenly become more difficult and even appeared a little mundane in comparison to the European fixtures. Filippo had settled in Madrid and the Gaffer was finishing his Slow Food book. For the 2008/09 season the team settled back into the London Midweek League, now competing with teams representing Merrill Lynch, an investment management company, Davis Langdon, a global construction company and Visa, the multinational financial services corporation. It was some way from 'Slow Foot' and situationism, but at least they held their own on the pitch, enhanced by some new signings and regular performers. Damian Evans was now the centrepiece of the defence and brought with him new players to add to the experience of Vipul Bhakta. Andy Finnerty was one of the regular players who kept the team going in this period, his reliability surpassing that of his employers Transport for London; rush hour Tube hold-ups and delays often led to a frantic dash from Maida Vale station along Randolph Avenue to reach the ground before kick-off. The German striker Conrad Mummert was the most impressive of the newcomers, scoring 21 goals in 17 appearances, and the team finished a respectable mid-table with 44 goals scored in all and 51 conceded.

It was not enough to convince the Gaffer that this was the future of PFFC, and at the end of that season the team was withdrawn from the London Midweek League to return to Sunday football and Regent's Park in what was a new and enlarged Grafton Millennium League, still run by the effervescent Barry McNamara who was happy to welcome them back. There were some familiar faces with Grafton FC and Falcons (now called Sporting Falcons) as well as a host of new teams and even a cup competition. There was no sign of Inter Aztec and therefore no repeat of the classic encounters of the previous years. PFFC's last two seasons in that league had brought consecutive titles but there was little possibility of reviving those successes, despite more promising recruits. A low mid-table finish, which included some heavy defeats to the now revitalised Falcons, was uninspiring and indicative of old problems of consistency and availability with 35 different players used in 14 league fixtures. The team seemed to be drifting back to their early days in the relative obscurity of the Sunday league, complete with hammerings, a little bickering and long pub inquisitions. That was until an email arrived from the writer-in-residence at the Whitechapel Art Gallery.

Brown's party comes out on top – but in a whole different ball game

Sally O'Reilly was starting a new project and had come up with the idea of a 'three-sided football match'. Three-sided football was the creation of Asger Jorn, the Danish situationist, artist and philosopher who in the 1960s had voiced reservations about the durability of the 'two-sided' class analysis of orthodox Marxism. His alternative theory was to be demonstrated through a football match in which three instead of two teams played each other on a hexagonal pitch (with three goals). The winners would be the team which conceded fewest goals, a condition which was supposed to instigate 'situations' on the pitch, consisting of tactical alliances, cooperation and collaboration. As the matches developed, shifting allegiances – depending on the score – would create a new dynamic, even a new 'dialectic', in Marxist terms. O'Reilly needed teams to test her ideas and a suitable occasion on which to launch it. She invited Philosophy Football FC, along with two other teams from the University of the Arts and a collection of graphic designers, to participate in a game that was to be played during the 2010 United Kingdom general election campaign. The idea was to represent the three main parties: PFFC, in their customary red (and with the former leader of Camden Council Raj Chada in the ranks), would be representing the Labour Party.

Three-sided football appealed to PFFC as a new challenge, and it would be one that would drive the club's priorities over its final years. Zurich had reawakened the situationists' ideas of the 1960s and 1970s; now there was an opportunity to put them into action. It was the chance for PFFC to take its philosophy on the pitch to a new level. In fact, a completely new approach was needed. The first dilemma was the serious practical one of ensuring that the pitch specifications met the hexagonal design. Goober Fox, custodian of the PFFC website, put together a brief layout and after much negotiation with O'Reilly and the other teams, a date and time was arranged for it to take place at Haggerston Park in Hackney. The second problem was to agree the rules. Asger Jorn was an artist-philosopher and not a footballer and although the game had been played on odd occasions, finding the precise rules on throw-ins, goal kicks and corners (and if so, who takes them?) was difficult and not completely resolved until the kick-off. How many players in a team? What should be the duration of the game? Two halves, or three? Should there even be referees, given this was partly about organised anarchy? If not, how are rules to be enforced – by collective consensus or spontaneous voluntarism of the aggrieved party?

In the event, and despite Asger Jorn's hope that the 'bi-polar' structural constraints of contemporary capitalism (partly dependent on the illusion of a neutral referee) could be 'deconstructed' by triolectics, the match started with two referees – manager Geoff Andrews and chairman Hugh Tisdale. The first five minutes went smoothly enough, with Luigi Coldagelli (once again travelling from Rome) providing the cross for fellow Roman Mauro Campana to head past the goalkeeper in the 'Conservative' goal. Headed goals would be a rarity in future three-sided games, mainly because (unlike in this first fixture) the goalposts were smaller. Shortly after, Matt Prout made it 2-0-0, before another Labour onslaught on the Tory goal resulted in an unusual predicament for the officials, with claims for handball bringing the first moment of indecision between the two referees. Claims for handball brought the first moment of indecision between the two referees. The second moment followed immediately after they had decided to award the penalty: who should take it? This was decided in favour of the last team to touch the ball before the handball, which happened to be PFFC. In normal Sunday

League circumstances this might have provoked strong reactions, but no more than mild curiosity was aroused as both officials pointed to the spot, or at least where, on a hexagonal pitch, they imagined such a point might be located. In any case Coldagelli's spot kick was saved. In PFFC's first three-sided match, their experience against two hastily cobbled together outfits probably counted for the victory, as they defended stubbornly to come away with '0' in a 2-3-0 victory, combining with the Tories to put three past the Liberal Democrats. It was to be Labour's only victory during the election campaign which ended with a coalition government between the Tories and Liberal Democrats, an alliance that prospered only briefly on Haggerston Park.

PFFC now had a taste of the three-sided game, which had attracted some local interest, with the *Hackney Gazette* and *East London Guardian* carrying enthusiastic coverage of the 'election-themed' demonstration of the 'beautiful game'. While intrigued about the 'philosophical judgements' that might emanate from having two referees, the latter suggested that PFFC had 'looked beyond the boundaries of the sport' in taking up the idea. It had all gone well, but a new intake of players was required if a three-sided campaign was to be sustained. Once more, another stream of adopted Londoners with a strong passion for football and a desire to play for a 'different kind of team' came on board.

Will Errington, introduced to the team by Jez Bray, had previously turned out in the West Lancashire League for Poulton Town and in the Blackpool and Fylde Sunday Alliance for various teams, combining right-back on Saturdays with central midfield on a Sunday. This versatility, together with his technical ability and sheer enthusiasm for playing whenever and wherever he could, proved to be a big asset to PFFC. Matt Prout was the second Cornish-born player to join PFFC. His first games of football at the age of nine were on the fertile agricultural slopes of the Tamar Valley on the Devon–Cornwall borders. From there he took his boots to the even wetter climes of West Wales, though this came to a brief halt while studying international relations at Aberystwyth University. After taking a job in the former Department of Energy and Climate Change, Prout went on to study for a master's degree in environmental and business studies at Birkbeck College, where he encountered the writings of the college's most famous son (and one of the Gaffer's old gurus) Eric Hobsbawm. Hobsbawm's observation in *Nations and Nationalism* that 'the imagined community of millions seems more real as a team of 11 named people' had by now found its way on to a Philosophy Football shirt. Joining PFFC's own ecosystem, Prout brought a committed environmental dimension, often spending the Saturday before matches planting tree saplings across London for the charity Trees for Cities.

Like Errington, Prout quickly developed an expertise for the three-sided game. He would be the most regular member of the squad when it extended three-sided football to Europe. His Sundays had normally been divided between PFFC in the morning and his beloved Plymouth Argyle Supporters' XI in the afternoon. However, by the time PFFC exported the three-sided game abroad, he was a seasoned traveller, living for a while in Malawi while working with Voluntary Service Overseas on climate change projects. With the three-sided game now prioritised in PFFC's commitments, it was still important to keep meeting as a regular squad. The 11-a-side team continued playing in the Grafton League to variable success. Training had never been a priority for PFFC – some players had joined on the explicit assumption there wouldn't be any – and despite the best coaching efforts of David Phillips, another Liverpool-supporting player, who took some summer evening sessions before returning north to start a career as a football journalist, it was enough to get 11 bodies on the pitch.

Public relations consultant Andrea Giannotti, another Italian import with a passion for British Sunday football, a former school-mate of Ricci and Coldagelli at the politically lively Liceo Mamiani in Rome, was now the main organiser of the weekly games at Regent's Park, assisted by Ally Clow, who after taking on the burden of looking after the squad when Filippo and the Gaffer were away, was now occupied in running a cinema. One of Giannotti's first moves was to establish the three centre-back system that was then employed successfully by Juventus and the Italian national team. In adopting a similar system, PFFC inserted its own three Italians – Giannotti, Michele Martinelli and Mario Gerace – at the heart of its defence. The GMG replicated the BBC of the Azzurri – Barzagli, Bonucci and Chiellini. Martinelli was another passionate 'Romanista', making AS Roma the second -most supported team after Liverpool among the PFFC ranks. Gerace was a landscape architect and introduced a colleague, Henry Duck, to PFFC. In the next few years, while Gerace was helping to hold PFFC's defence together in 11-a-side fixtures, Duck became a leading participant in their three-sided campaign.

Ömer Çavuşoğlu was another new player recruited in this period. He was working at the London School of Economics attempting to analyse different urban configurations when a colleague, Atakan Guven (also briefly on PFFC's books), put him in touch. He was PFFC's first Turkish player, and had grown up in Istanbul supporting Besiktas. Though he had not played 11-a-side football in Turkey, he had taken part in an early experimental form of the game at his high school which was played on a semi-circle base of an amphitheatre. Three individuals or three teams of two would play with two of the goals directly facing each other, with the third in the middle, on the outer rim of the semi-circle. Three-sided football reminded him of that earlier experience. Joining PFFC three years after moving to London, the team was a key part of his immersion into London life, as it was with so many of the players. PFFC, in its three-sided phase, appealed to him because it offered a truer sense of football played not only with muscles but, as he saw it, with brains.

***

Unsurprisingly, the first of the European tournaments and the first three-sided game on Spanish soil was held in Madrid, where Filippo had extolled its merits among his coterie of football correspondents. He loved the anarchistic nature of the game, the quickly changing dynamics, in which (for example) blue-shirted midfielders pass to red-shirted attackers against white-shirted defenders and – not least – the apparent invisibility of the referees. The PFFC strip for the occasion of their 17th international tour was suitably anarchic, internationalist and philosophical: the blue strips displayed the Monty Python commentary leading up to the only goal in the Germany v Greece international football match.

'There's Archimedes, and I think he's had an idea! "Eureka!" Archimedes, out to Socrates. Socrates back to Archimedes. Archimedes out to Heraclitus who beats Hegel. Heraclitus a little flick. Here he comes, on the far post. Socrates is there. Socrates heads it in! Socrates has scored! The Greeks are going mad! Socrates scores! But a beautiful cross from Archimedes. The Germans are disputing it. Hegel is arguing that the reality is merely an a priori adjunct of non-naturalistic ethics. Kant, via the categorical imperative, is holding that ontologic exists only in the imagination, and Marx is claiming it was offside.'

Opponents were the X-Men, the former PF Madrid team of journalists Filippo founded after arrival in the Spanish capital, who wore white Albert Camus shirts, and a team of Spanish existentialists dressed in the black Jean-Paul Sartre shirt. The game was played in the neighbourhood of La Elipa, scene of the award-winning comedy *Dias de Futbol* ('Football Days'), in which a group of friends found new motivations, meanings and friendships in their troubled lives through seven-a-side football.

The match produced a spectacle and a surprise for the many three-sided debutants, who were initially suspicious of what they thought were over-complicated and intricate rules. In fact, the fast-changing nature of the game and the need for quick-thinking tactical alliances brought flowing moves and good camera shots of white-shirted strikers converting a blue-shirted cross. Over the duration of the three halves, the X-Men, to the delight of captain Sid Lowe who became an enthusiastic convert to this form of the game, triumphed in a 3-5-5 victory. The first three-sided tournament in Spain had won admirers, and three weeks later the second three-sided match in that country was hosted by the Athletic Bilbao Foundation by writer Galder Reguera.

In the next international three-sided football match in Rome six months later, it was the turn of PFFC to stage a remarkable comeback, turning around a 4-4-1 scoreline to win 4-6-7 against local opponents Sant'Onofrio and Real Fettuccine, who had visited London two years before, with Prout and captain Coldagelli in good form. PFFC's team, in addition to Prout, Joe Boyle and a welcome return for Marco Capecelatro, was made up of veterans and youngsters with Filippo having recruited a brother born in the 1950s and a nephew born in 1997. The two Roman teams showed a distinctive reluctance to abandon the classic two-sided game. There was an ominous clash between the strong winning mentality that the Italians famously apply to football with the triolectic idea of three-sided football. For them, it wasn't proper football. This was in sharp contrast to the Spaniards, who being more used to a less serious idea of football and a more entertaining approach to the beautiful game, were able to enjoy the match and quickly absorbed the philosophy of the three-sided variant. The match was played at the historic Donna Olimpia pitch, in the borough of Monteverde, a former haunt of PFFC favourite Pier Paolo Pasolini, who lived from 1954 to 1959 in Via Fonteiana, just in front of the pitch, and then in nearby streets until 1964. It was in

Monteverde that he conceived his famous novel *Ragazzi di vita*, based on the street boys of a poor working-class district.

The tournament was partly a celebration of Geoff Andrews' 50th birthday (with the PFFC players wearing shirts covered with his optimistic words – 'Un altro calcio è possible' ('Another idea of football is possible') – but it coincided with an equally important event for him at the time, namely the final departure from office of Silvio Berlusconi, who had dominated Italian politics for the previous two decades. It was a double celebration, interspersed with meals and news interviews and ended on return to London with a lively debate on the *Jeremy Vine* show. His rival on the line from Emilia Romagna was Nicholas Farrell, a 'revisionist' historian and resident of Mussolini's hometown of Predappio, who, along with Boris Johnson, had a few years earlier interviewed Berlusconi for *The Spectator* where the latter claimed Mussolini 'had not killed anyone' and described Italian judges as 'mad'.

Three-sided football was flourishing, and as PFFC expanded their involvement with this form of the game – regularly receiving enquiries from reporters who were fascinated by its novelty and quirky rules – more requests were received for matches and tournaments. This included the Basque Country. Shortly after he arrived in Spain, Filippo met Galder Reguera who ran the cultural programme of the Athletic Bilbao Foundation and every year since 2009 he has organised Letras y Fútbol, a festival that combined books and football. Before each festival Reguera selected five club members, the manager, two players from the first team, a player for the women's team and a director, and asked football supporters, not only Athletic fans, to advise them on what books to read. Reguera put down a list of five titles for each of the Athletic members and they picked one title. Once they had read it, they discussed it on stage during the Festival, initiating a unique series of encounters and round table discussions. Reguera is also responsible for the Thinking Football initiative: a film festival dedicated to football which started in 2013 and in which for a week several films from all over the world dedicated to football are shown, for free, in Bilbao's cinemas. Reguera regularly invited Filippo to intervene at both festivals, but the most precious call came in 2012, when Reguera asked him to bring PFFC to Bilbao to take part in a three-sided game to be played in the prestigious Vistalegre Plaza de Toros, one of the most famous bullrings in Spain.

More negotiating, galvanising and cajoling from Filippo had produced a spectacular venue and a serious collaboration with La Liga's Athletic Bilbao, who had been promoting three-sided football within their foundation and club structure. During the official 2018 World Cup, Galder Reguera and Carlos Marañon, director of the Spanish magazine *Cinemania*, son of a former Espanyol and Real Madrid player and author of the acclaimed book *Futbol y Cine*, embarked on a dialogue that was later published in the book *Quedarà la ilusion*. Marañon mentioned Filippo and told Galder a few days before the official tournament began that he had previously been a World Cup winner. Recalling the story, Marañon said that he had participated in a three-sided tournament in the Elipa district of Madrid and had won it. He thought that that was the first three-sided encounter ever played in Spain, and Galder confirmed, 'It annoys me a bit, but I must admit that Filippo was the first to actually organise a three-sided game here in Spain. He beat us here in Bilbao by one month. Filippo, who has played three-sided football in different countries and with people of various nationalities, says that it's a game that allows us to know the idiosyncrasies of different cultures, that people from one country tend not to break an ally whilst others will betray you at the first opportunity, and only because the game allows you to do it.'

The 2012 tournament was played in June and was comprised of the Athletic Bilbao Fundazioa team (composed of pupils and teacher of the famous Athletic's football formation school) and Internacional FC Santander, a team based in the Cantabrian city and made up of immigrants from different African countries, who were decked out in the blue and white hoops of Queens Park Rangers. On the gravel-covered pitch in the shadow of the circular amphitheatre structure of 10,000 seats, PFFC lined up with Mather, Giannotti, Prout, Errington, Patrono (from Rome), Ricci and Ian Coyne, who had disrupted a family holiday in Biarritz to join the squad after a long absence. The quality of players on each side was high: Internacional FC were playing in a semi-pro competition at the time and were physically in a league of their own, though their knowledge of three-sided football was limited, resulting in a tight and exciting affair with high quality goals and an ongoing drama which extended to the last of the three halves. In fact, the final score of 6-6-6 was a tie and only resolved by Filippo's introduction of what became known as the 'Basque' amendment to the rules of three-sided football which dictated that in the event of a draw the side who had scored the most goals would be the winner. In this case it was Santander Internacional who came out winners. This spontaneous improvisation, along with the replacement of the hexagonal with a circular pitch, may not have appealed to the Asger Jorn traditionalists but was indicative of the anarchic side to the game as it evolved on the pitch.

Three-sided football was now being talked about more widely and PFFC started to receive more press enquiries about its implicit critique of the commodification of football; this critical side was something Andrews and PFFC had long sought and now, finally, seemed to be within reach – hexagonal pitch and three goals notwithstanding. People were noticing and were curious. Coaches, interested in improving the tactical side of their training, got in touch hoping to learn more. It appealed to growing numbers of mixed gender teams. At one PFFC game in Regent's Park in May 2013, dubbed the 'biggest three-sided tournament to have taken place in the UK', *The Guardian* reported, 'There remain no rules beyond a handful of basic principles: the pitch must be hexagonal in shape and equally divided into three, halves can last for any length of time, teams can vary in size, there are no offsides, and goal kicks, throw-ins and corners operate on the basis of each team having two sides on the pitch: if the ball goes out on either of your sides you get the set piece; if it went out off you, it goes to the team whose goal is nearest to the ball.'

Invariably, initial curiosity of the journalist – in this case Sachin Nakrani – was how such enjoyment and competitiveness ('joviality' he called it) can be derived from apparently complex or contrarian principles. 'It is organised confusion,' Filippo told him. 'It's a synthesis of football, basketball, chess and poker,' according to Mark Dyson, one of the original three-sided footballers from the London Psychogeographical Association who had played in the first known three-sided match in the UK at the Glasgow Anarchist Summer School in 1993 and was the most knowledgeable exponent of the game who would shortly set up the first three-sided league in London. 'There is an obvious increase in complexity but essentially it's two-sided football with an element of bluff. It's utterly unique and people who play it, love it.'

'At a time when there is a worry about the commodification and corporatisation of football this brings back the true essence of the sport,' Geoff Andrews, who had waited a long time to identify a concrete example of his club's philosophy on the pitch, pointed out.

10

Jumpers for Goalposts
in Taksim Square

WITH THEIR three-sided adventure now consuming all their efforts, the next triolectic tour was equally ambitious and – in the initial planning – not without its dilemmas. With the exception of Prague, the tours to date had been in western Europe, often aided by knowledge and contacts of at least one of the main participants. News of PFFC's three-sided exploits had travelled and in May 2013 Geoff Andrews received a message out of the blue from Thomas Buesch, a German film director based in Istanbul. How about a game here, he suggested? It would coincide with the international art *biennale* in September. Buetsch and his partner were involved with InEnArt, a hub for international as well as community-based artists and which, together with Diyalog, an Istanbul-based non-governmental organisation, sought to bring together artists, curators, academics and a network of cultural organisations. In short, Buesch saw it as an opportunity to spread the counterculture through the medium of three-sided football and in the spirit of Asger Jorn.

The invitation became even more intriguing over the next couple of months as protesters occupied Gezi Park and other locations in central Istanbul. The demonstrations started as a rejection of planning proposals for the park but extended to an attack on the authoritarian government of Prime Minister Recep Tayyip Erdogan, for his crackdown on alcohol, public kissing and even the shouting of political slogans at football matches. The protests quickly spread throughout Turkey, causing a brutal backlash from the government who attacked demonstrators in Istanbul's Taksim Square and other central locations.

'Things are getting interesting in Istanbul,' Beusch told Andrews. The biennial art exhibition had also picked up on the rising discontent and titled the exhibition 'Mom, am I barbarian?', borrowed from poet Lale Müldür's book, which identified with the displaced status of the stranger or foreigner. The other choice, 'Taksim Everywhere', was banned by the police. As the focus of the exhibition was to be on the topical theme of public space as a political forum – a hugely contested issue in Erdogan's Turkey – the search was now on for a suitable venue for the tournament. For Buesch the ideal place to hold it would be Gezi Park or Taksim Square itself. However, Erdogan had clamped down on all public protests and, as Beusch told Andrews and Ricci, 'It is quite possible that first the civil police will show up and after 40 minutes the nearby anti-terror units will show up with pepper spray, helmets and truncheon, to stop our activities.' The prospect of having the game curtailed and players arrested – while an appealing situationist tactic – was rejected on British utilitarian principles. Another shortlist was drawn up which included two parking lots and a square next to Gezi Park, and a smaller, tree-lined park.

Finally, Beusch and his colleagues came up with an artificial grass pitch on a public park on the Golden Horn, near to the biennial venues. Fortunately, it was on ground owned by Kadir Has University. Behind the pitch the university museum was hosting an exhibition titled 'Joyful Wisdom', which at least gave hope to the players. In the publicity for the tournament, Beusch described three-sided football as an:

'Artistic form, a "spectacle" and the chance to demonstrate that different views, ideas and approaches can be expressed freely and spontaneously in ways that promote dialogue and cooperation rather than conflict and division. We see it as offering a positive contribution to the recent protests in Turkey, at the same time sharing the broad ideals of the 13th Istanbul Biennial, and an innovative way to portray artistic freedom and dissent. Furthermore, the three-sided football match in Istanbul will focus on the theme of public space as a political forum following the protests of the last months in Turkey.'

The other two teams involved were to be Dynamo Windrad from Germany and Ayazma Football Club from Turkey. Though sadly without Ömer Çavuşoğlu, their one Turkish player, PFFC's squad included – together with three-sided regulars Clow, Duck, Prout and Patrono – Mark Dyson, who the previous year had founded the Deptford Three-Sided (later Luther Blissett) League. Dyson was concerned about the pitch measurements. It was to be the shortest pitch in the history of the three-sided game which also created difficulties in setting out the hexagonal dimensions.

Most of the squad arrived from London on a flight that went via Kiev with Ukrainian Airlines. Duck flew in from Dubai and Patrono from Rome where he was now working for RAI 5, the cultural channel of Italy's main broadcaster (he would make a documentary about the tournament on his return). With accommodation near to the Grand Bazaar, the squad acclimatised to the city by wandering around its passageways of trinkets, carpets and shoes, and later by the discovery of a Galatasaray FC supporters' bar. The evening was spent with hosts Thomas Buetsch and Asena Heyal of InEnArt and some of their opponents, in a restaurant overlooking the Golden Horn. The wine flowed that evening; on the other visits to cafes and restaurants during the trip the squad demonstrated that a football team on tour doesn't always need alcohol to enjoy great food (but it helps).

In fitting with the protest movement, the tournament was preceded by a 'slogans workshop', which attempted to reconcile the situationism of the 1960s with the prevailing conditions in Turkey. After the more reticent philosophers had been out-shouted by their opponents, the tournament referee, Halil Ibrahim Dinçdag, who had been sacked by the Turkish Football Federation in 2009 on grounds of his sexuality, got proceedings under way. A large crowd assembled and witnessed a tight affair – not only by the narrow margins of the final score but also because of the congested playing area. Boyle and Clow theorised that if the two sides of the hexagon were lengthened more room for playing could be consolidated in an unusual (and irregular) lozenge. This was a spontaneous revision that met with Mark Dyson's approval, and the match commenced in a strong spirit of friendship.

The match kicked off with a pink ball and PFFC, in resplendent red shirts adorned with 'Mom, am I barbarian' (the title of the art exhibition) and playing in a 1-2-1 formation in the tight arena, won the tournament 5-6-10 (with Duck excelling); perhaps an indication of their greater experience of this form of football. After the game, all the teams were presented with their 'medals' by the Turkish artist Genco Gulan; the medals, in fact, were bananas with the words 'Golden Horn' inscribed on the skins, an appropriate gesture for an event organised in association with the Istanbul Biennale.

The tournament was played in a welcoming atmosphere and after the preliminary concerns about interference from the state, it was free of any involvement with the police. After the match Beusch and Heyal hosted a party for the teams in their central Istanbul apartment overlooking the Bosphorous, where more ideas and cultural projects for extending the three-sided game were discussed over beer and music. Just after 11.30pm, the cartoonist Tan Cemal Guric, who had produced an animated trailer for the tournament, escorted the squad to the centre of the city where they could at least get a view of the contested spaces where they had originally planned to hold the tournament. Now, approaching midnight, they arrived in Taksim Square where in the apparent absence of a large police presence, the players decided on an ad hoc 'jumpers for goalposts' three-sided game in one corner. Local bystanders joined in (even the Gaffer came out of retirement) and seemed to quickly pick up the rules (more evidence to refute the charge that the game was overly complicated). PFFC had got to play on Taksim Square after all, and the occasion was given a further lift when an elderly man, walking across the square, put his finger to his nose and said (in English) to the players, 'I smell freedom.'

With the smaller three-sided squad meeting only once a month and the 11-a-side team continuing to play more regularly, there was a constant need to replenish the squad. Goalkeepers were always in demand and veteran keeper Rob Adams was now looking after the three-sided team, so the recruitment of Kadeem Simmonds was an important addition. Simmonds was in his final year at university in

Brighton when he met Ally Clow at Wembley Stadium while working on Raise the Flag – the 'fan-friendly', FA-backed initiative of Mark Perryman and PFFC chairman Hugh Tisdale to promote fair play at England international matches. Clow quickly cottoned on to the fact that Simmonds was a goalkeeper, and it was soon a done deal once the latter had moved back to London permanently. Expecting a typical Sunday League team, Simmonds found that instead of the familiar 'dressing room banter' heard everywhere across the country first thing on a Sunday morning, there was a bit of 'politics, the state of the world, philosophy. Of course, there was talk of what we hoped to achieve over the next 90 minutes, but it was always insignificant to the wider reason as to why we were there, to have fun.'

The main concern for Simmonds, and James Ferdinand who joined the team with him, was the prospect of playing in t-shirts (even ones beautifully designed by Tisdale) rather than a 'proper' football kit. But ultimately that was overcome, as was the long journey from his home in east London for the 11-a-side fixtures. He settled quickly, made some saves, and had never had so much fun playing football. He won player of the year in his first season. Since returning to London, Simmonds had worked at McDonald's and Next before becoming the sports editor of the *Morning Star* (the first black editor of a national newspaper).

In May 2014, Simmonds joined the rest of his squad for the inaugural Three-Sided World Cup in Denmark. This was organised with the help of Mark Dyson, Dynamo Windrad and the cooperation of the Museum Jorn in Silkeborg (Asger Jorn's hometown) which houses his artwork, and now hosted the first football tournament in his name. It featured nine teams of five players (three substitutes allowed), composed of three from the UK, including two PFFC teams (PF England and Jorn Three) and Mark Dyson's Republic of Deptford; two from Silkeborg (one made up of former Superliga players, plus the Silkeborg YMCA); and one team each from Poland, France, Germany (Dynamo Windrad) and Lithuania (where a recent three-sided tournament had been held), which for some reason played under the Uruguayan national emblem.

Prior to the tournament, and instead of the slogan competition that had opened the Istanbul event, a more formal seminar was held at the museum on the legacy of Asger Jorn and his significance for three-sided football. Mark Dyson excelled in his elucidation of Jorn's key ideas and what the wider world can learn from triolectics; Andrews contributed some thoughts on the continual evolution of his squad and its prolonged attempts to unite philosophy and football on the pitch; and others helped raise the intellectual level by theoretical interventions and lively anecdotes from their own experiences. It was surely the first football world cup preceded by a day of theoretical and artistic inquiry and raised expectations of a complex tactical tournament.

On the back of its Istanbul performance and other victories, PFFC entered the tournament as favourites, though that status was quickly eclipsed by the experienced Danes who defied the growing belief that you can't win three-sided football matches on technical skill alone. The Lithuanians, one of several mixed teams of men and women, lived up to their anarchist principles: they were less interested in winning football matches than disrupting other games and attempting to change the rules of the tournament midway through. The tournament had not only three halves but three dimensions: the initiators (which decided the ranking); the heats, and the final. Jorn Three, the younger of the PFFC teams (including Simmonds, Ferdinand, Prout, Errington and Mather), did make it to the final by knocking out PF England along the way to face the two Danish teams. Rivals throughout the tournament, they were now able to combine more effectively as allies for much of the game – which was briefly disrupted by a Lithuanian anarcho-syndicalist streaker – with Silkeborg YMCA taking the trophy, 1-5-7.

Three-sided football now became PFFC's modus operandi and subsequent seasons were spent in the Luther Blissett Three-Sided Football League in Deptford, in less competitive but more convivial fixtures. Curiosity in the game grew rapidly and after 2014 TV cameras were a common sight at Fordham Park, with journalists often participating as players to better understand its dynamics. Luther Blissett has never been impressed with his reincarnation as a symbol of the anarchist left, and though now it is common for managers, players and pundits to discuss their team's 'philosophy', in general professional footballers have been far less enraptured by philosophy than philosophers have been with football. Philosophy Football had learned the hard way that if you want to win football matches then there must be a compromise: ideologically rigid positions don't pick up the spare man at the far post or deal with pacy, in-swinging free kicks. Likewise, while three-sided football often encourages greater respect for passing and movement it can often lack the competitive edge, and the quality of the football at Deptford was not always the highest.

This tension between its football and philosophy had been there from the earliest days of PFFC. Occasionally it had caused dressing room rifts, misunderstandings and disagreements (sometimes continuing over prolonged email exchanges), but also lots of new ideas and projects. It had delivered new experiences and unusual opponents, while offering regular football in a weekly competitive league which brought a purple patch of three successive championship trophies. However, that tension between philosophy and football returned in its last big event, the 2018 Unofficial (Three-Sided) World Cup, held in Madrid the week before the official two-sided tournament in France.

Once again Filippo had found a unique pitch for the tournament in the form of another bullring and was beginning to line up some interesting opponents who had been won over by his enthusiasm for this form of the game. However, some of the hardcore 'three-siders', including the Lithuanian anarchist faction who played at Silkeborg, as well as some of the original pyschogeographers, found the idea of a tournament in a former bullring in conflict with their principles. The spokesman for the Abra Cadaver squad (as the Lithuanian anarchists now called themselves) declared that at such a venue the tournament should be dedicated to the 'dead human, non-human and the more than human workers of the world'. In such a place, it was important first and foremost to demonstrate that harming any living being was wrong, and 'to respect living, dead, productive, non-productive, psychic, reproductive and even destructive labour and not to care about such abstractions as capital'. Any attempt to distinguish the Unofficial World Cup teams on the grounds of nationality was also to be rejected, since the 'strict demand for clear affiliation to name, kit and anthems is closer to nationalism than to working-class solidarity'. In fact, it was argued that to organise the tournament along anything resembling normal football was itself a breach of the sacred principles (as they saw it) of the three-sided philosophy. Filippo, who had spent much time finding players, negotiating between teams, arranging accommodation and dealing with the venue staff, was exasperated by the voluminous and antagonistic email exchanges.

'This is a football tournament,' he reminded them. 'We will play football. If you come with other purposes, situationism, strike or other bullshit, please stay at home.'

His words drew a furious response from Abra Cadaver and their allies. He was told to 'retract' his statement and called a 'liar … who speaks with the corpse of Franco in his mouth'. Andrews, who came to his defence, was dismissed as a 'Stalinist' for agreeing that the tournament needed to have rules. In fact, the tournament itself was now denounced as 'fascist' and 'sexist' (and presumably 'speciesist').

This was now too much for Filippo, who decided to call off the tournament two weeks before it was due to begin, with travel tickets already booked and accommodation arranged. It was only when the other squads, including the

Germans of Dynamo Windrad, rallied to his defence that he agreed to carry on. Abra Cadaver continued to berate the organisers as 'bourgeois conspirative reactionaries' who had 'sided with FIFA'. Despite the possibility of the tournament being disrupted, Filippo went ahead and the PFFC squad travelled once more to Madrid.

On the morning of 2 June six teams entered the little green door of the San Sebastian de los Reyes bullring, on the outskirts of Madrid. The 'plaza' is known as La Pamplona chica, the little Pamplona, as its design is reminiscent of one of the most famous *plaza de toros* in Spain, the one celebrated by Ernest Hemingway. The teams represented four countries: Dynamo Windrad, now Trinamo Windrad, from Germany; PFFC and New Cross who had arrived from England; the local team, Sanse, guided by Angel Fernandez, a talented Spanish forward who had played for PFFC in London a few years before; and another Spanish squad composed of the journalists of *Marca*, the leading sports newspaper. Another squad was RoMad, an international formation composed of Italians, Spanish, British and Irish players, with the regular guest player Luigi Coldagelli joining Sid Lowe, Carlos Marañon and Rodri Errasti (who with the last two had been on the winning side in the previous three-sided game in Madrid in 2011).

In the same squad were a couple of Romans (Marco and Simone), an Irish keeper and an important late recruit. Stefano Sorrentino was then the first-choice goalkeeper with Chievo in Italy's Serie A. He was on holiday in Madrid with his fiancée and had called Filippo, whom he knew from his time in La Liga with Recreativo Huelva. The two had remained friends and over tapas Filippo asked Stefano if he fancied adding the three-sided game to his football portfolio. Sorrentino liked the idea and joined the RoMad team, while Filippo went on to play with the mixed German team, made up of two women and four men including the extraordinary goalkeeper Alex Grijelmo, 62 years old and a well-known Spanish writer. Although Grijelmo did not win the Three-Sided World Cup trophy he would take the prestigious Premio Castilla y Leon de Ciencias Sociales y Humanidades that year. Filippo also proudly provided two more members of his family for PFFC: his nephew Isaiah, who had already worn the philosophical shirt many years before in London, and his son Gregorio, by now 15. Greg was the sixth member of the Ricci family to take the pitch for PFFC in 18 years. The PFFC line-up at the Gaffer's disposal was completed by Clow, Clarke, Prout, Boyle and Julian Jaen, a Spanish photographer and part-time goalkeeper.

Calcio a tre porte, sudore e filosofia "I gol si fanno usando il pensiero"

A hotly contested, friendly tournament was enlivened by some gentle anarchism, which now seemed integral to the whole idea. The final was between RoMad, Marca and Trinamo Windrad. The first two had tied in the number of goals conceded, but instead of playing ten more minutes they preferred to take penalties. Filippo wanted the game to continue, as he considered it philosophically – and most of all 'three-sidedly' – much fairer, as the third team (his team in this case), even if defeated and with no chance of lifting the trophy could still have played a decisive part in the remaining minutes by forging an alliance or betraying an ally with the other two contenders. However, 'the "Latin" spirit prevailed', as Filippo saw it; Latin in this sense meaning that will to win, that competitiveness, that *cattiveria agonistica* that he so badly wanted to transmit to PFFC back in 2001. Italians, always, and, to a lesser degree, Spanish players, have it in their genes. And it prevailed in the 'Little Pamplona'. Sorrentino, the Serie A goalkeeper who had played outfield for the whole tournament, finally put on his gloves: not only did he score his penalty but saved the last one of his opponents, enabling RoMad to lift the alternative World Cup with Coldagelli netting the decisive spot kick. Fewer than ten weeks later Sorrentino would save another penalty: the one taken by Cristiano Ronaldo on his debut for Juventus in Serie A. Sorrentino couldn't finish that game because of concussion suffered after a too close encounter with the Portuguese star, and Chievo went on to lose 3-2 at home. That was bad luck for the three-sided world champion.

Once more three-sided football had left a vivid impression, both of football and philosophy. This was best summed up by Carlos Marañon, who reflected on the tournament and on his second three-sided win after that of 2011, in conversation with Galder Reguera in their book *Quedará la ilusión*, 'The feeling of playing a sport that you already know but with different rules is really curious, it takes you to your childhood, it gets to you from the inside, from

your infant side, giving you the pure pleasure to play. At the same time you find yourself in trouble, facing different difficulties but, as you know how to play, it becomes a kind of challenge and it brings you to rediscover an ancestral link with the ball that is transmitted and shared with your team-mates. We were like children having a great time. And yes, it was different and not only for the location *"taurina"*. It was really funny, and on top of that we won all the games, final included.'

Epilogue

Football Comes Home

WE ARE back where we started: San Basilio, Rome in 2005.
PFFC are in the final of the tournament having swiftly
dispensed with the Italian film directors 4-1. In the final,
PFFC had the upper hand against the Pasoliniana when
Clarke stormed into the opposition's penalty area, was

tripped, stumbled, regained his balance and shot straight at the keeper.

It was a decisive moment in the match, and after surviving that chance the actors recovered and went on to win the tournament on penalties.

Back in the PFFC dressing room, a debate ensued.

'Why didn't you go down?' Clarke was asked.

'It was a clear penalty. We would have won the match!'

'But that would be diving. Well done Clarkey, for staying on your feet,' one of his team-mates responded.

'At the end of the day it was bad luck. Win some, lose some.'

'It wouldn't have been a dive. He was fouled. It was a clear penalty!'

'But it's not really ethical, is it, to win like that. Anyway, it's only a game.'

The discussion continued at the post-match dinner and into the evening in Rome's bars. It became a post-mortem. It was *the* turning point. If only Clarkey had gone down. But wouldn't that be cheating? It was football versus philosophy: the 'results business' set against the pure joy of taking part.

That there was a debate at all was a reflection on how the team had changed since the moment earlier in its history when Filippo 'went down a bit too easily' and was chased off the pitch by opponents, with his embarrassed team-mates looking on sheepishly. PFFC had taken his Italian mentality on board and had learnt how to win. There were three consecutive championships and, despite San Basilio, several European trophies to show for it.

This transformation in PFFC's mentality co-existed with a wider shift within the domestic football culture, evident in England's route to the final of the 2020 European Championship. Indeed, according to *The Times*'s football correspondent Henry Winter, one of the country's leading football writers, when Raheem Sterling won the controversial penalty against Denmark in the semi-final, it was English football's 'coming of age'. These 'successful tactics', Winter argued, 'revealed the streetwise streak instilled in age-group teams by FA coaches over the past seven years and now manifesting itself in the senior side'. This, he went on, was the preparation they needed ahead of the final against Italy. In short, there was a growing view among the English media that the national team had displayed the streetwise (or, we might add gently, cheating) attributes of the Italians. This legacy was long debated among the PFFC WhatsApp group, as the English players discarded their runners-up medals after their defeat to Italy in the penalty shoot-out, and Italian fans were chased out of Wembley by irate English nationalists.

Filippo became engaged in the debate, reflecting on his earlier experiences in London. It was a troubled recollection. In the aftermath of the final, he published a thread on his Twitter account that became very popular and generated an insightful debate. As usual, he wrote with passion, as was always the case when he reflected on England, London and the *calcio inglese*.

'I feel the need to say something about England,' he began. 'A country I grew up admiring, a country I lived in and loved. A country I now find difficult to understand.

'Let's stick to football. Why the entire world supported Denmark and then Italy? Cause the English approach and communication around the beautiful game is unbearable, fastidious, old. They keep explaining a game they don't understand, and the few things they've learnt came from the bloody foreigners. The reading of the papers yesterday was unnerving and painful: I felt for all those colleagues that filled pages and pages with hope and despair, patriotism and broken hearts, talking about revenge without a line on the opponents, an analysis of the defeat, a football critical approach. The emptiness.

'And now let's go back to Sunday [the final]. The violence, the drunkenness, the danger, the anger, the racism. I watched in disbelief how thousands of people entered Wembley without a ticket. That 70s feeling. The authorities denied, the witnesses confirmed. The approach to the football games of the national team in England has not changed through the years. It's still a matter of conquest. England travelling fans' behaviour is appalling: they invade cities, put flags on the monuments, drink in an unpleasant way, can't hold their piss, they look and thrive for a fight, they're menacing and never joyous. No one else does that. They felt authorised, and they're not. At home they fight between themselves, they throw bottles and find it funny. They whistle the opposite national anthem and whistle their players who take the knee. And the Prime Minister don't condemn those fans. The same fans that racially abuse their players. Because they're racists. Everyone knows that, but no one dare to say it.

'There's a minority of fans that is horrified by all this. But they've no voice. Cause if you say something you lose your patriotic passport. The media approach to the tournament and to the final was following the same line. The cheaters are now streetwise, the prose full of Englishness, the empire ready to strike back. I found it annoying and surpassed. I think England has to look at his football from a totally different angle. Why there are not black fans following the national team? Why it's accepted to behave like hooligans? Why the national team inspires the worst from fans? This Euro will go down as a lost chance.'

Filippo felt a little deceived: he had this sincere and deeply held love for the '*calcio inglese*', the English football he had witnessed from 1976 to 2021, a passion that had been taken to a new level with PFFC. Yet it was also true that in the 1970s the Italian admiration for the '*calcio inglese*' developed also into a worrying flirtation with the violence on the terraces. In Italy, a country divided by the political violence of the 'years of lead' for almost 20 years, football hooliganism was depicted as 'fascinating' and 'intriguing', studied in sociology courses, and somehow transformed by the left-wing intellectuals into the class struggle. The Heysel tragedy in 1985 changed everything for supporters, but Filippo recalled that when he started to report on English football from London in 2000, he still found a good number of Italian colleagues with a 'soft spot' for hooliganism. Twenty years later, among the top five European leagues, Italy is the only one that still has a kind of reverence for the Ultras movement, one that has a big and unresolved problem with football violence. Filippo was very clear that Italy was in no position to give lessons on the subject, but he felt 'betrayed' by the fact that hooliganism still plays a part in English football when the national team is involved. What disappointed Filippo most was that the violence at Wembley was a million miles from his more recent experience of life with PFFC. The club went abroad, the club played in London, welcoming players from all over the world, blending experiences, histories, cultures, visions, habits into one football field. It was inclusive, never exclusive.

At the same time as Filippo was airing his concerns on Twitter, the Gaffer wrote an article for *La Stampa*, one of Italy's main newspapers, entitled 'A Disunited Kingdom'. Here he contrasted the scenes at Wembley and its aftermath with the image of a youthful, multicultural symbol of modern England that was cultivated and reinforced by England manager Gareth Southgate. This modest, mild-mannered man, sometimes compared to a geography teacher, instilled in his team a strong camaraderie, more tactical awareness and removed the individual egos that had plagued the team in the past. Some of the players – Jadon Sancho, Kieran Trippier and Jude Bellingham – had even benefited from wider European experiences, playing in La Liga and the Bundesliga. Egos which flourished in the past were not allowed to affect the squad, and the values and personality of the manager, a decent, honest and hard-working student of the game, appeared to be ingrained in the squad's ethos.

But Southgate had a lot on his plate. This was now an England at the centre of a very disunited kingdom. The divisions following the Brexit referendum of 2016 continued to define its politics and culture (including football). Brexit was also followed by increased support for independence for Scotland (which voted against Brexit) and Wales (which voted for it). Many Scottish and Welsh people supported Italy in the European Championship Final on the grounds that Boris Johnson (like Silvio Berlusconi in Italy) would exploit a victory for political reasons.

For many, Southgate's England has stood as an example of another country, of what England could aspire to be. Many on left and right in politics exploited the situation. A Conservative MP refused to support England's football team if it continued to 'take the knee' in its protest against racism while others exaggerated Southgate's press statements to imply that he was attacking the government. Yet the real strength of Southgate's 'Dear England' open letter to the nation, composed before their first tournament match against Croatia, was its appeal beyond the political divide. He recognised the sacrifice and heroism of the doctors and nurses during the pandemic, of 'the fragility of life' and of the pride of representing his country. Off the pitch he embraced patriotic values and offered a vision – or perhaps a glimpse – of a more united country.

On the pitch, he also hinted at a different England. Gone were the long balls and the unchangeable 4-4-2 formation, where talented individuals were forced into unfamiliar positions. Instead, there was more emphasis on tactics, with Southgate changing the team to suit the opponent. Kalvin Phillips and Declan Rice, the two defensive midfielders (a position long neglected by England), became more important.

As Italians understand better than anyone else, football has the capacity to reflect wider values, divisions, hopes and aspirations beyond the game. This was never more evident than in the case of the England national team in the post-Brexit era of a pandemic. Southgate did his best. It was not enough to win the tournament or, perhaps in the end, to unite the country. His stated desire in 'Dear England' that 'every game, no matter the opposition, has the potential to create a lifelong memory for an English fan somewhere', was not ultimately realised in the final itself.

Over 20 years, PFFC had made a similar cultural shift, from Sunday League regulars to a squad composed and sustained over the years by the London diaspora. This was the diaspora that had changed many lives and made new dreams possible for many, including professional sportsmen and women like Emma Raducanu, the 18-year-old tennis player who won England's first women's Grand Slam title since 1977 when she triumphed at the US Open in September 2021. This was a girl born in Toronto to a Romanian father and Chinese mother but brought up in south London since she was two years old.

The city's diaspora was crucial to PFFC's identity too, and its capacity to draw in players from six continents and 24 countries. 'PFFC made me British,' Ömer Çavuşoğlu, the Turkish-born player, recalled. 'In its internationalist, non-pompous but proud, embracing way. Sacrificing many Saturday nights for soggy Sunday mornings was all worth it.' PFFC offered a home for those new to London. For Italians Mauro Campana and Lele Capurso, the team helped them settle in a new country while, following Filippo, their 'Italianness' contributed to PFFC's developing identity. When he arrived in London from Preston, Owen Mather knew only his two house-mates, but PFFC 'provided a ready-made network of like-minded friends in an unfamiliar and huge city that I knew relatively little about'.

PFFC's players came to London for work. The team offered escape from the drudgery of routine by stimulating camaraderie, convivial occasions, and lifelong friendships. It also enabled them to travel and imbue a strong dose of internationalism, matured over 23 European trips and 24 nationalities. Uniquely, PFFC enabled a group of people from different backgrounds and walks of life to come together where in normal circumstances they would never have met. Raj Chada, defence lawyer of left-wing causes, did the tackling and ball carrying so that his midfield partner, His Honour Judge Alan Johns QC, who normally adjudicated on business and property cases, could go off on mazy dribbles. Lele Capurso, an amiable, soft-voiced Italian doctor training at Hammersmith Hospital, was, for a season, one of PFFC's most vocal players, constantly demanding more effort from the London transport employee, retail salesperson, musician, teacher and lawyer he had only just met. If PFFC often provided an escape from work – that joy of the Friday night flight out of London – for some players, it even influenced the day job. Being PFFC captain at 23 taught Ally Clow, a Scot who had moved south in his early 20s, 'how to speak to, motivate and (sometimes) bollock a disparate group of people', which he found to be invaluable preparation for managing staff at Curzon Cinema in Shaftesbury Avenue.

Rob Adams, veteran goalkeeper, Penge resident, and latterly custodian of the three-sided squad, reflected on his long PFFC career, 'I doubt there are many individuals who will play grassroots football for a number of years with such a variety of souls and with whom you feel such a natural affinity. It's hard to put into words what exactly playing for PFFC gave me. I suppose the main aspect was enjoying the game with people who tended to have the same approach to life. The outlook was truly internationalist and incredibly unique and has given me firm friendships well into my middle age.'

The players had come to London for work, and the team had given them a home. It also took them to Europe. For Kadeem Simmonds, who like many joined the team without knowing what to expect, 'It was like nothing I had experienced, and I know I never will again. Being introduced to three-sided football and playing in the first World Cup in Denmark will probably rank as the highlight. I remember that weekend perfectly. Stepping off the plane in Denmark to play in a World Cup, wandering round to view the landmarks with the team, it was magical.' The team embraced Europe at the time when the UK's fractured relationship with the continent was being played out in the shadow of Brexit. That most of the players became convinced Europeans was born from practical experience, with football as the linchpin. This made them Europeans. For Joe Boyle, 'It was thrilling to play football with Italians, Swiss, Hungarians and to travel for ecstatic weekends to play in lofty venues in European cities.' Alan Johns, mercurial winger, *bon viveur* and barrister, only started travelling abroad after he joined the team. 'We all embraced internationalism and we drove the relaunch of three-sided football as an alternative form of the game,' Ally Clow recalled.

In the end, what probably kept PFFC going for so long and what united a disparate group of players was this European identity. The team discovered the practical benefits of European integration, embraced its cultural mix, and shared histories through the different footballing traditions. This kind of ordinary Europeanness was missing from the lacklustre Remain campaign (and its successor, The People's Vote) during and after the referendum on the United Kingdom's membership of the European Union, which, in the views of some squad members, had treated Italy and other southern European countries harshly. On the pitch, they learned a new language of how to play, to communicate and (sometimes) to win. Off the pitch, they were drawn to the cultural possibilities that opened up before them; to experience at first hand Europe's foods, football, and nightlife; occasionally its politics.

If the club had become European and was troubled by the Brexit campaign, then it had mellowed in some of its political ambitions. Yet, in its last period, football and politics converged to remind the club why it had been founded and had managed to sustain and refine its appeal to a growing band of part-time players. Firstly, the announcement by a group of elite clubs – elite by power and wealth rather than league positions – that they were setting up a European Super League reflected everything that PFFC abhorred. It was the clearest statement yet that corporate elites ruled football, saw themselves above the law and that the values of fair play – the elite clubs could not be relegated in the new league – was secondary to the pursuit of profit. The feelings and principles attached (for example) to the 'magic of the FA Cup' had diminished. The Gaffer's idea expressed in a shirt worn on a PFFC three-sided match in Rome of 'Un altro calcio è possibile' ('another idea of football is possible') had been pulled apart by corporate interest. In Italy and Spain, the fight against 'modern football' in recent years converged around a slogan, 'Odio eterno al calcio moderno', ('I hate modern football') and the Super League represented all the worst fears: the negation of any possibility of an upset, and the denial of the kind of dream that in the spring of 2021 brought Villarreal from a city of 50,000 inhabitants to defeat Manchester United in the Europa League Final.

Ironically, the Super League madness was halted by the Premier League clubs. This was not according to the principle of defending grassroots football or any 'magic of the cup' but only for economic and self-interested reasons. UK Prime Minister Boris Johnson played a part in the dissolution of the Super League in the frantic uproar it generated over 48 hours, and subsequently England was rewarded by UEFA, which moved more European Championship games to London, with the possibility of filling up Wembley during the Covid pandemic. Meanwhile, in Rome and Seville, Italy and Spain were playing in front of crowds of just 15,000 supporters; an audience limited by strict Covid protocol.

And this is the same football elite that in December 2010 granted the 2022 World Cup to Qatar. Enquiries and trials about corruption preceded and followed the vote and the tournament was moved from summer to winter.

Amnesty International denounced the conditions of the workers who were employed to build the stadia, and *The Guardian* in February 2021 revealed that no fewer than 6,500 migrant workers had lost their lives in the period since Qatar was awarded the World Cup. This World Cup, the greatest football tournament, will be watched live by a very limited number of supporters because of its timing and location. And the same FIFA that assigned these finals to Qatar has lobbied heavily to organise the World Cup every two years. More games, more money, more business. The fans no longer matter.

The swift collapse of the European Super League, with one club after another announcing its resignation from the project, was testament to the strength of feeling throughout the football community. Nowhere was this more evident than in the UK, where fans, ex-players, club officials and pundits (in an unusual display of wisdom), together with interested politicians mobilised oppositional opinion to the proposals. It seemed as if football had, at least partially (and

temporarily) recovered its soul. It also meant that the ideals of PFFC were not so different from the mainstream, and that change could happen from within. After more than 25 years of tours, tackles and tactical manoeuvres football had, by the end, displaced politics 'as the art of the possible'.

The threat of a new European Super League will not go away and the spectre of the Qatar World Cup is ominous. The almost 30 years of PFFC may not count for much in the big scheme of things. Looking back from the vantage point of 2022, many questions remain – above all, would PFFC have been possible after Brexit? – but we stand by our philosophy. And it has been a blast.

Player Profiles

Rob Adams

It was the acrobatic heroics of the 2000/01 season that earned the Penge stopper the famous 'Rob the Cat' nickname rather than his 2003 attempt to scale the window ledges of Pordenone after he had locked himself in (and out). Known to quote Ibsen at advancing centre-forwards, he was the complete philosopher-footballer between the sticks. Still turns out in the Luther Blissett Three-Sided League.

Kieran Alger

Sweat, tackles, shouts, headers, long-distance shots: Alger epitomised the qualities of English football (at least for someone who comes from the continent). The Devonian twice captained PFFC on overseas tours.

Joe Boyle

Reliable right-back, capable of regular forays into the opposition half as well as some memorable last-ditch defending. A committed Europhile, as PFFC's most regular scribe his legendary match reports evoked the dramas and tragedies, the flaws, spirit and humour of the squad from Regent's Park to Rome.

Jez Bray

A regular in the 2000/01 season, it was PFFC who turned him into a European citizen. Firmly embedded into the European Community in Brussels since 2001, he continued to turn out on European tours when his French was useful in the bistros of the *rive gauche*. The scientific expertise of this reliable right-sided midfielder was called upon by the president of the European Commission during the Covid-19 pandemic.

Mauro Campana

Ponytailed forward known in the outskirts of the Via Cassia in Rome as 'Neeskens' or 'Bomber', he contributed to the PFFC cause with a bone of his nose (when attacked by a rival team) and some valuable pieces of play. Another thinker addicted to music, this DJ and music producer converted from midfielder to forward on the Gaffer's request.

Marco Capecelatro

The first of the Marcos, and the one with the most impact on the team. As Filippo launched his assault on the club's mentality during the title-winning 2001/02 season, Capecelatro led the cultural revolution on the pitch. His role as the team's first number ten inspired his team-mates to play better football, while his movement and technique brought confusion and uncertainty to opponents. Though his time with the team was short, his legacy was immense.

Lele Capurso

Doctor Lele stormed into the team, and almost immediately to Loftus Road too, in PFFC's winning season of 2003/04. He arrived through a long and winding road (as brother of a friend of Filippo's wife) but left a great mark on and off the pitch bringing character, humour, and unity to the squad, while uncovering a talent pool of players at Hammersmith Hospital.

Ömer Çavuşoğlu

PFFC's only Turkish player and lifelong Besiktas supporter. Ömer Çavuşoğlu, an academic at the London School of Economics, was always interested in the philosophical side of the game. This made him a vital player and loyal ally of fellow Arsenal supporter Rob Adams in the monthly triolectics of the Luther Blissett Three-Sided League.

Paul Clarke

Brought to the team by chambers colleague Alan Johns, 'Clarkey' made his mark for PFFC in their first Grafton championship season. Infrequent appearances over the next couple of years were followed by his now legendary performance in Sicily in 2004 where he completed an extraordinary day of stolen wallets and lost luggage with a match-winning performance on volcanic ash in the hills beneath Mount Etna.

Ally Clow

As the youngest captain of PFFC, the Scottish musician and film aficionado took on multiple roles for the club. Though mainly a pacy midfielder who could operate on either flank or down the middle, when needed he also appeared at full-back and in defence. Captain, secretary, and chief negotiator during the torrid months at Hackney Marshes, he was a protege of the Gaffer, and a loyal exponent of the club's ethos on and off the pitch.

Ian Coyne

Another football journalist, who originally brought Filippo to PFFC, 'Coyney' played in every position in the team from goalkeeper to centre-forward. Most at home at centre-back where he was a towering presence at the heart of PFFC's championship-winning teams in the Grafton League. Known for getting lost in London, he had the habit of finding the top corner from 30-yard set pieces.

Will Errington

Errington joined the team in the same period as Prout, and was another standout performer in the Bilbao bullring. Technically adept and versatile, he was equally at home in defence or midfield. Another product of the strong Lancastrian component of the squad, he had unfailing devotion to his native Blackpool despite their slide from Premier League to the Championship.

Damian Evans

The first Welsh captain of the team and the perfect heir of Paul Kayley in the heart of the defence. With the former skipper he also shared the honour of the best defender in the history of PFFC. Reliable, fast and cool, he managed to revive the almost defunct playing career of Filippo by 'running for two'. Voted as players' player of the year in 2005, he's the first (and only) non-Roman Roma fan of PFFC.

Stefan Howald

Voted the one and only 'player of the decade', he made his debut for the team in his early 40s as a founder member of PFFC and went on to be a model of professionalism. Despite his age, his pace remained one of PFFC's main attacking threats for many years. As host of PFFC's first tour, he started its European adventure while his writing gave PFFC a niche readership in Switzerland.

Neil James

Breaking all PFFC's goalscoring records in the 2002/03 season, with an astonishing 40 in 13 games (including eight in one match), the rugby-mad Kiwi occasionally enticed his team to do the Haka before kick-off. Unsurprisingly, he was always being lured back from retirement at times of need, before emigrating to Canada where he still keeps in touch with his former team-mates.

Alan Johns

Better known as 'Cornish Al', he signed for the club on the basis that he would never have to participate in any form of training. Influenced by the Christian philosophy of C.S. Lewis, he also went through a conversion on the pitch with the occasional tackle and header. Skilful winger, and loyal servant of the club (motto, 'In God and Gaffer we trust'). Adept at adding Frank Sinatra to the PFFC playlist.

Paul Kayley

The club's most successful captain, Kayley had to wait a long time for his first win in a PFFC shirt. An admirably convivial team player as an Evertonian alongside many Liverpool supporters, he nevertheless refused to wear the Shankly shirt throughout his career. As the partner of many centre-backs of different shapes and sizes, his cool authority and constant encouragement of his team-mates was vital to the team's championship glory.

Owen Mather

Once the youngest and sometimes the wildest, Mather ended his career, older, wiser and the most capped player in PFFC's history. An incredible parable: from boozy nocturnal messages on the Gaffer's answerphone to the position of esteemed treasurer, and from crunching tackles and cards of various colours to an irrepressible late career as reliable, back-up goalkeeper.

Matt Prout

Another, like Clow, who joined the team as a talented young player and went on to play a key role in the life of the club; in his case as the most capped and star performer in the three-sided format of the game. His technical ability and relentless energy (he thought nothing of turning out for PFFC in the morning and Plymouth Argyle Supporters' Club in the afternoon) was vital, as was his enduring commitment to PFFC's philosophy.

Kadeem Simmonds

Came to the club via Raise the Flag, the FA-backed initiative of Mark Perryman and Hugh Tisdale (and scouted by Ally Clow), and quickly made an impression between the sticks. His PFFC career rapidly reached the heights of the Three-Sided World Cup Final and players' player of the year, at the same time as his journalistic career took off.

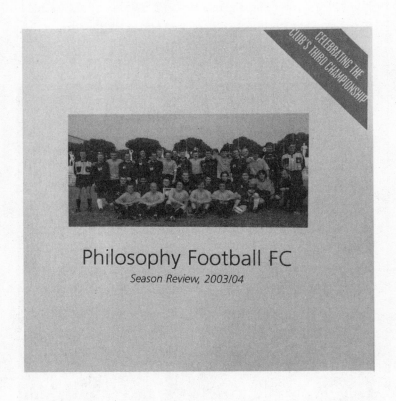

CELEBRATING THE
CLUB'S THIRD CHAMPIONSHIP

Philosophy Football FC
Season Review, 2003/04

LA PARTITA DI PIERPAOLO

Campo Francesca Gianni
Via Casali di San Basilio, Roma
29th October 2005
From 2.00pm

Teams:
Osvaldo Soriano FC ● Philosophy Football FC
Pasoliniana ● Nazionale Registi

30 *anni dopo*
Pasolini
u n o t r a n o i

Comune di Roma

The cities we visited in our Tours

Zurich 2000

Rome 2000

Prague 2001

Pordenone 2001

Parisot 2001

Brussels 2002

The Hague 2003

Casarsa 2003

Rome 2004

Sicily 2004

Paris 2005

Rome 2005

Madrid 2006

Lisbon 2007

Bra 2007

Zurich 2008

Madrid 2011

Rome 2011

Bilbao 2012

Istanbul 2013

Silkeborg 2014

Madrid 2018

The nationalities of our players

Australia
Bulgaria
Canada
Chile
Denmark
England
France
Germany
Ghana
Greece
Hungary
India
Ireland
Italy
Mexico
New Zealand
Nigeria
Poland
Portugal
Scotland
South Africa
Spain
Switzerland
Turkey
USA
Wales

The pitches we played on in London

Battersea Park
Clapham Common
Crystal Palace National
  Sports Centre
Dulwich School
East Ewell
Ferndale Road Sports Centre,
  Brixton
Fordham Park
Hackney Marshes
Haggerston Park
Hampstead Heath
Hampton Court
Holland Park
Leyton Leisure Centre
Linford Christie Stadium
Malden Road

Marble Hill Park, Richmond
Market Road
Mile End Stadium
Motspur Park, New Malden
Paddington Rec
Perivale Sports Ground
Ravenscourt Park
Raynes Park Sports Ground
  Hurlingham Park, Putney
Regent's Park
Royal Festival Hall
Spitalfields Market
Wandsworth Common
Wandsworth Park
Wapping Sports Centre.
Weavers Fields
Wormwood Scrubs

Acknowledgements

THE AUTHORS thank Benedetta Mascalchi for her wonderful photographs that feature throughout this book. We are grateful to Stefan Howald for sharing his diary comments on the early years of PFFC; to Joe Boyle for editorial suggestions, to Goober Fox for producing our annual PFFC review and looking after our website, and to Hugh Tisdale, designer and co-founder of philosophyfootball.com, for ensuring that we were the best-turned-out team even when we lost. We enjoyed the hospitality and help of numerous people on our tours and their invaluable contributions are discussed in these pages. Finally, we thank the more than 250 players who turned out for PFFC for their enthusiasm, commitment, conviviality and good humour. This is their story.

Also available at all good book stores

9781801500470

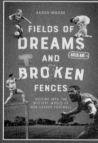

9781801501002

9781801500586

9781801500739

9781801501149

9781801500913

9781801500968

9781801501101

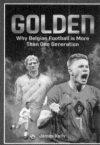

9781801501057